PRAISE FOR G

"*Godly Dating 101* is a call for all singles to put Christ at the center of their dating lives, measuring everything they do and say to each other against what Christ did for them. How do we keep a gospel-centric perspective in a world full of lies? With passionate personal stories and practical scriptural references, the Greys help to expose cultural lies as well as help us experience true biblical conviction that leads to a vibrant, authentic, and God-honoring relationship that will last. Their hopeful approach will help you to see dating as not just a relationship you should try to keep healthy, but also one that should help make you whole and holy—in every situation."

—Rashawn and Denisse Copeland, Founders of Without
Walls Ministries and Social Media Influencers

"I have dedicated my adult life to help people date well in the church, and that is why I am so excited about this book! Tovares and Safa use scriptures, their experiences, and real-world situations to guide you in dating God's way. By picking up this book, you gain a curriculum to Godly Dating 101."

—Jonathan Pokluda, Bestselling Author of *Outdated*,
Host of *Becoming Something*, and
Pastor of Harris Creek Baptist Church

"If you or someone you know is trying to successfully navigate the world of dating, love, sex, and marriage, get this book! Tovares and Safa speak biblically, candidly, and practically on these crucial topics, providing a much-needed resource for Christians everywhere!"

—David Marvin, Director of The Porch and Author of
We're All Freaking Out (and Why We Don't Need To)

"Tovares Grey has given a lot of dating advice over the years, helping many people to avoid the pitfalls that can come with the tricky road of relationships. More importantly, he helps you to do it God's way. This book needs to be a go-to guide for every follower of Jesus who wants to date well."

—Matt Brown, Evangelist, Author of *Truth Plus Love*, and Founder of Think Eternity

GODLY DATING 101

Discovering the Truth About Relationships
in a World That Constantly Lies

TOVARES & SAFA GREY

W PUBLISHING GROUP

AN IMPRINT OF THOMAS NELSON

Published in Nashville, Tennessee, by W Publishing, an imprint of Thomas Nelson.

Unless otherwise noted, Scripture quotations are taken from the Holy Bible, New Living Translation. Copyright © 1996, 2004, 2015 by Tyndale House Foundation. Used by permission of Tyndale House Publishers, Inc., Carol Stream, Illinois 60188. All rights reserved.

Scripture quotations marked BLB are taken from The Holy Bible, Berean Literal Bible, BLB. Copyright © 2016 by Bible Hub. Used by permission. All rights reserved worldwide.

Scripture quotations marked CSB are taken from the Christian Standard Bible®. Copyright © 2017 by Holman Bible Publishers. Used by permission. Christian Standard Bible® and CSB® are federally registered trademarks of Holman Bible Publishers.

Scripture quotations marked ESV are taken from the ESV® Bible (The Holy Bible, English Standard Version®). Copyright © 2001 by Crossway, a publishing ministry of Good News Publishers. Used by permission. All rights reserved.

Scripture quotations marked KJV are taken from the King James Version. Public domain.

Thomas Nelson titles may be purchased in bulk for educational, business, fundraising, or sales promotional use. For information, please email SpecialMarkets@ThomasNelson.com.

Any internet addresses, phone numbers, or company or product information printed in this book are offered as a resource and are not intended in any way to be or to imply an endorsement by Thomas Nelson, nor does Thomas Nelson vouch for the existence, content, or services of these sites, phone numbers, companies, or products beyond the life of this book.

ISBN 978-0-7852-9301-9 (TP)
ISBN 978-0-7852-9302-6 (eBook)
ISBN 978-0-7852-9303-3 (audiobook)

Library of Congress Control Number: 2022935068

Printed in the United States of America
22 23 24 25 26 LSC 10 9 8 7 6 5 4 3 2 1

To Zion and Gianna, our children who we love more than words. You are our biggest motivation. May you become who God destines for you to be and not who culture expects you to be.

CONTENTS

INTRODUCTION

In 2012, my brother Glenroy and I (Tovares) were very active on Twitter. We loved sharing truth and addressing difficult subjects. We formed an account called Anointed Misfits because we felt that truly described us: two guys who loved Jesus and weren't afraid of backlash.

I realized that as I posted the things God would lay on my heart regarding dating, we would get a massive amount of feedback. Many young adults began to ask questions and asked us to address certain topics. After my brother stopped posting, I kept the page going because I saw that this was something that could possibly shift a culture. After some time in prayer, Godly Dating 101 was born. I sometimes look back and think God must have a sense of humor to allow a twenty-year-old male to create a page that would encourage relationships God's way. Not because a young person can't do great things for God, but because I still battled lust and was single while telling people how a God-honoring relationship should look.

Godly Dating 101, however, was on God's heart. Growing up in the church, I paid attention to the way we addressed the convenient conversations but ignored the difficult subjects. Dating was a topic most leaders avoided. I found it amazing that I could be in church approximately five days in my week but not hear anything about relationships. Unfortunately, the church remained silent on many of these issues, giving worldly culture a chance to be vocal on what to do, how to do it, and whom to do it with. So many lies were taught to us that are still normalized today.

After speaking with hundreds, if not thousands, of individuals over the years, I have learned that people genuinely have questions about dating. It grieves my heart when I see individuals turn away from their walks with Jesus to find relationships, or when I see people who are honestly not happy with their relationships but settle for the abuse or poor definition of love they're experiencing just so they won't be alone. I believe that the person God will lead us to will strengthen our faith and reassure us to stay connected to Jesus, but modern relationships aren't prioritizing God in their relationships. Our Bibles inform us that God is love, so we know He should be the example of what true love is (1 John 4:16). But we so often hear about relationships from ungodly sources and people who aren't speaking what the Word of God declares. Many brothers and sisters are being pressured into being high-value men or women who are every man or woman's dream. People have developed expectations on what to look for in "the one," but no one will address the fact that God has certain expectations for us to follow if we want a relationship that honors Him.

When Tovares and I (Safa) started dating, I wasn't aware of this ministry that he had created. If I had had any idea beforehand, perhaps I would have declined his pursuit. Not because he didn't fit my ideal of what a husband should be, but I didn't think that I could be bold enough to minister on such a large platform. I have always had a burden for helping young ladies walk into their God-given purpose. And through Godly Dating 101, God has enabled me to do just that and has cultivated a burden in me specifically for helping people navigate confusion in regard to dating and purity. As in my home church, I knew I was called to ministry in a special way; I just thought it would be on a much smaller scale. But God said, "Safa, think bigger." Godly Dating 101 has been that bigger picture for me. I realize that many women run into the same issues that I faced while single and aren't sure where to go for answers. This ministry has allowed us to teach many followers of Christ that it is okay to be set apart for God's purpose and that they can date in a way that honors Christ.

What if we told you that God isn't as quiet on relationships as you may have thought? That even if your church hasn't prepared you for marriage, the Word of God is clear on how you can prepare for what you're praying and waiting for? Over the past ten years, the online ministry of Godly Dating 101 has grown—now run by us (Tovares and Safa) as a married couple—and has connected to millions of individuals who genuinely seem to have the same goal of honoring Jesus in their relationships.

When responding to emails from young adults all around the world, we find that so many seem to be asking the same questions.

"Should I go back to an ex?"

"Is the Bible really against pornography?"

"How do I know if this person is the will of God for my life?

"Will I ever get married, or am I called to singleness?"

What if we told you that dating doesn't have to be so hard? There is no reason you should try to navigate the opinions of everyone other than Jesus. Life isn't always simplistic, but you must understand that the Word of God is a reliable source for you to learn from as you're seeking to know whom to marry and whom to avoid. Psalm 119:105 says, "Your word is a lamp to guide my feet and a light for my path." As you read this book, our goal is to show you what the Word of God says about relationships and to remove the misconceptions that culture has taught you.

Through this ministry, God has taken many people out of sinful relationships, reassured millions of their worth in Christ, and caused many to decide they will never settle again. We are passionate about showing others that God loves them too much to give them a relationship that doesn't help them spiritually and emotionally. As amazing as marriage has been for us, our greatest blessing has been how much we can help each other flourish in who God destined us to be. It's our commission and privilege to show others who they are in Christ and encourage them to live a life that honors God. We want to reassure this generation that you are not weird and your standards are not too high simply because you choose to obey the Bible. You can date in a way that pleases God, and we are the proof that God wants to do great things in your life and in your relationship without you having to compromise or follow in society's footsteps.

GODLY DATING IS PREPARATION

FOR MARRIAGE

A couple of months into our marriage, I (Tovares) decided I wanted to make Safa a special Italian dinner. I thought it would be quite romantic because of how much she loves Italian food. I had never really attempted to make lasagna before, but I decided it was time to treat her to a gourmet meal at our fancy home-restaurant that for one evening would be called "Casa dei Greys."

I told Safa not to worry about anything that evening. I wanted her to sit back and relax and trust that I had it all taken care of. I sincerely believed that I had all the information I needed to cook up a meal as good as anybody on Gordon Ramsay's *MasterChef* show. Once I prepared this incredible meal, Casa dei Greys was surely going to be sponsored by the Food Network. Needless to say, YouTube cooking videos and I became best friends the week prior as I prepared for that special evening. I'm not too proud to admit that I was obsessed with Pinterest for food ideas. But what do you expect? I didn't see Italian meals that often growing up in a Jamaican household.

First, I went to the store and bought all my ingredients. Well, at least I believed I had all the necessary ingredients for a wonderful Italian dinner. I bought the beef, parsley, various types of cheese, and tomato paste, and for the rest I simply thought I'd use what we already had in our pantry. The day finally arrived and I was getting ready to cook the meal. My wife, with her compassionate heart, realized that I had no idea what I was doing. These days I aim to do most of the cooking in our home, but back then when we were first married, Safa handled preparing the meals. It was clear to her from observing at a distance that she needed to step in or I was going to burn down the apartment complex. Boy, was I relieved to get some help!

Safa looked over at me and asked the question that seemed most obvious to her. "Babe," she said cheerfully, "so, where's the actual lasagna?"

I looked back at her, confused, but wanting to seem on top of things. "I'm making it now." That may have been the moment when she fully realized the man she married had clearly never cooked an Italian dish in his entire life. She scanned the kitchen counter again and still didn't see the lasagna. She went on to patiently explain to me that lasagna is actually a particular type of wide-stripped pasta. I thought lasagna was all about cheese and beef. Clearly you guys can tell that the closest I came to eating Italian food was the one time I went to Olive Garden and only ate their bread and a salad. But I reassured her with irrational confidence that she was mistaken and those strips weren't necessary. They were only needed to make the dish look fancy. My pride simply wouldn't allow me to admit I wasn't making any sense. I continued to put together the beef and ricotta cheese on top of each other without the lasagna strips. I carried on with this stubborn charade for nearly an hour before I realized that no matter how good my intentions were, without the right preparation and ingredients, the outcome would never be the way it needed to be.

The one question at the front of everyone's mind whenever I share this story is, of course, "How did the lasagna recipe without lasagna actually taste?" I'd like to preserve a little pride here, so I'll just say I'm thankful that we lived near a great pizza restaurant so I could take Safa out for a well-cooked Italian dinner. Without the right recipes, ingredients, and preparation, "Chef Grey" here was only fit for cooking shows like *Kitchen Nightmares.*

I share my cooking disaster because in many ways preparing for marriage is similar to preparing a great dinner for someone we love. Our preparation has a direct effect on the outcome. We can pay attention to the details ahead of time to make sure we are ready for the experience. We can research and find the right recipes from the best cookbooks. We can shop to make sure we have all the best ingredients available.

We can plan out each step of the dinner, having everything from the right kitchen tools to the perfect candles and place settings. The time and attention you spend in preparation for that event will help your chances of having a successful gourmet cooking experience. In the same way, when it comes to marriage, we cannot allow ourselves to go into it without the proper preparation.

I don't believe it's possible to ever be fully "ready" for marriage, because there will always be trials, tough days, and moments when you may even find yourself begging God for patience to stop you from bickering. But just because you don't know what lies ahead doesn't mean you can't be more prepared for it. If you are single, now is the moment to prepare for the relationship you desire. You want to be ready when God opens that door. Failing to prepare is like trying to create a gourmet meal without doing what you need to do ahead of time. Use your current season to align yourself with God's will.

START BUILDING NOW

Whenever I think about planning, I think of one Bible character in particular who saved humanity by sticking to a plan. Noah was a man like many of us who was aiming to honor God in a society that was far from Him. Due to humanity's constant sin, God's heart began to grieve to the point that He regretted creating them. Despite most of the world's shameful actions, God saw that Noah was still a man who aimed to honor Him.

God told Noah that He was going to destroy the world by flood, and He gave him specific plans to build a boat that would save his family—and two of every animal. Can you imagine what people would think today if you quit your job, went into your backyard, and began to build a huge boat? When I think of how Noah responded to God's command, I'm reminded of how often I don't have my faith placed fully in God and His plan for my life. It's not because Noah was perfect and I'm a failure, but Noah was faithful despite not knowing *when* God was going to do what He promised. It's easy to build an ark when I see the rain clouds forming. It's easy to run and tell my family what we should do when the thunder and lightning begin to take place. But the Bible doesn't tell us that Noah started building once God sent the rain. The Bible mentions that Noah found grace in God's sight, and God gave him specific instructions on how to escape the impending judgment. Upon receipt of those guidelines, Noah began to execute God's plan down to the last detail. He followed the instructions exactly the way God commanded (Genesis 6:22).

I wonder what would've happened to Noah if he'd decided to just partially obey God. What if he'd built the kind of boat he wanted? What if he simply hadn't built the boat according to God's specs—maybe more like Carnival Cruise instead of what God said? No matter how much Noah believed God, his fate would've been the same as everyone else. It was his obedience that protected him and his family and allowed humanity to survive.

In the same way, if you apply certain godly disciplines to

your relationships now, it is possible to help divorce-proof your marriage before you say "I do." Again, marriage is one of those things that you can never truly be ready for. You may have an idea of what to expect, but it's not until you're there that you realize the joy and frustration that come with it.

Maybe you feel you've been in "good" relationships that ended poorly, but many times, I believe, we prayed for something that we never prepared for. Maybe you sought God diligently for a godly wife. You fasted for weeks, asking God to show you if this man was godly and "the one" for you. Despite our prayers, more goes into finding and being a godly spouse than simply praying for God to bring you someone who is perfect. With God all things are possible, but some areas in our lives require maturation and personal growth.

Our culture often says that we are to find "the one," and once this occurs, we will live happily ever after. Sadly, many have found godly partners and instead of riding off into the sunset, they've ridden off to the courthouse for divorces. Why? They assumed that finding the "perfect" spouse was all that was necessary for the marriage to flourish. Unfortunately, the perfect spouse doesn't exist; we all need God to work on us. If there was such a thing as a perfect spouse, they more than likely wouldn't want us anyway, because we aren't perfect. The goal isn't to find the perfect person, but to become someone worth pursuing—someone desirable because of how you carry yourself. So instead of ending up in divorce court, we should find ourselves ending up on cloud nine with someone God approves of instead.

BE WILLING TO CHANGE

When I was growing up, I learned something from looking at the relationships of grown-ups around me: the mindset that "they should take me as I am, and if they can't accept my flaws, then they can kick rocks." We've all met someone with that mentality. Maybe we are that person. The problem with that attitude is that it's lacking accountability. It lays the responsibility for making the relationship work on the other person, when really that was never their burden to carry. Why should they be obligated to deal with issues that we should fix? At the risk of sounding overly spiritual, "That's just the way I am" is a demonic mindset. That's because the Bible says when we are born again, we are new creatures in Christ (2 Corinthians 5:17). If the Word of God says I am a new creation and my old habits are now gone, then it's only our Enemy trying to convince us that we should maintain our flawed, sinful ways rather than allow God to make us new. We shouldn't say, "The one God has for me will overlook my toxicity." Yes, the person God has for you will understand you aren't perfect, but they should see you growing rather than being comfortable in immaturity or worldly habits.

We're often taught that dating is recreational—a way of turning people into objects of our satisfaction. But that shouldn't be the goal of dating. The purpose of dating should always be finding the right partner for marriage. Our hearts are too precious to God to simply give them to anyone. When you are dating someone, you are aiming to see if you can spend your life honoring God with them. Contrary to what culture tells us, marriage should be the main goal of dating, because you want to connect to someone in a loving covenant rather than date someone out of boredom.

While you are preparing for marriage, you may feel some of the same feelings Noah experienced while building the ark. Maybe he felt clueless, afraid, or anxious. But despite how he felt, he was just fine because he prepared the way God instructed him to. (Disclaimer: I don't want any of you to think that I'm saying marriage is like the disastrous, deadly, world-ending flood Noah was preparing for. If that were the case, I feel like God would have never ordained that union.) What I do want you to grasp is that when God has great plans for your life, you start working and preparing for it early. Let's talk about a few ways that you can start today.

HOW TO PREPARE FOR MARRIAGE

God sometimes places us through a process before He gets us to the promise. If we take a moment of introspection, we can find some flaws, habits, mindsets, and insecurities that will harm the future that we are praying for. I believe we are called to fix certain things prior to the marriage relationship to avoid stunting the growth we could experience as a couple.

1. EMBRACE YOUR CALLING

Growing up, my parents were strict on business before pleasure. They had no problem giving us the basic necessities you would expect parents to give their children, like food or shelter. But gifts and surprises meant we had to do something extra. We were expected to take care of our responsibilities first; they wouldn't reward laziness. Good grades meant being treated to a meal at our favorite restaurant or some new sneakers. Being respectful and keeping the house clean meant we could expect a new PlayStation game. If we didn't do our part, the only guarantee was that we would have a house to sleep in.

Whenever I hear someone expressing their desire for marriage, it reminds me of something God said in Genesis 2:18: "And the LORD God said, It is not good that the man should be alone; I will make him an help meet for him" (KJV).

What an amazing reward from God. I have no problem with that verse. I mean, who am I to argue with God? My issue is that we often quote that verse but manage to overlook what God instructed Adam to do prior to sending him that helper. We ask God for the promise, but we often neglect the process that He required prior to attaining it. God wanted to bless Adam, but Adam wasn't idle before God stepped in. Adam didn't set up a hammock and lounge about eating mangoes all day—though that's what I would've done in the garden of Eden, to be honest with you.

Genesis 2:15 says, "The LORD God placed the man in the Garden of Eden to tend and watch over it." Adam was given a mission before he was given a helper. He was told to maintain the garden. Not only was he told to watch over it, but he was given the opportunity to exercise dominion over everything that God created (Genesis 1:28). God gave Adam a purpose first and foremost. Adam was spending his time with God and doing what God called him to do.

What I find fascinating is that we don't see any verse where Adam asked God for a spouse. God saw that Adam needed company. So initially, God gave him animals to name. While Adam was saying which one would be the monkey and who was going to be the ostrich, God saw that Adam still didn't have a helper suitable for him. That is when God blessed him with Eve. It's interesting that when God saw Adam doing what he was purposed to do, Adam didn't have to request his own spouse. God saw that need before Adam ever realized he was "alone."

Of course, it's important to pray for a godly spouse because that would be a considerable benefit to your life. But God knows exactly what you need before you even decide to pray (Matthew 6:8). Often we ask God to send help before we start doing what God has created us to do. It's not as if the moment you serve God you will automatically meet your spouse, but I believe that many of us delay some blessings from God by simply not doing what He called us to do in our current season. Finding someone to marry is easy, but if we are to find the person God wants us to marry, we must be close to Him. We need to be close enough to see when He is saying yes or no regarding our choices. Close enough to know that we are in His will instead of following our changeable emotions. When we are abiding in His presence, we will experience clarity instead of confusion. We can be sure that the person we're with is a blessing to our life rather than a distraction that we chose out of loneliness or boredom.

I am of the persuasion that if you aren't first doing what God has called you to do, you shouldn't be pursuing a spouse. A little tough, but let me explain why. We've talked about how part of preparing for marriage is pursuing what God has called you to do. Why is this important? It helps us find our identity not in a human relationship, but rather in God first. Certainly pray for a godly man or woman to marry—but don't let your pursuit of marriage become a distraction from your calling. While marriage is beautiful and teaches us so much, our purpose on earth is far greater than marriage itself. God designed us all to do something for Him (and for others), and that should always be our top priority.

2. LOSE THE BAGGAGE

Our first argument in marriage was over the right way to prepare spaghetti. I told you Safa's love for Italian food is real! I was of the persuasion that one should mix the noodles with the meat sauce, since that was my habit. Safa believed it was better with meat sauce on top because that's how she was used to it at home or at Italian restaurants. In my immaturity I argued that she was wrong and my way was obviously correct. Eventually God had to convict me about approaching marriage with the mentality that my way was the right way, and she was in error for not being on board. Relationships may not fail because of spaghetti, but there is still much friction when we enter into a relationship with the wrong mindset.

Similar to the take-it-or-leave-it attitude I encountered in childhood, there's a trend across social media that informs people that the person they're with should "take them as they are," but that can be dangerous. The right relationship will surely help you heal from your past, but why is it your partner's burden to carry? I believe that in marriage we all need self-accountability (we will discuss this later). We can't come in expecting our mate to heal broken areas of our lives that can only change after we spend time with God. A brand-new relationship can make us happy, but it doesn't replace the baggage in our lives.

What are some things God is asking you to let go of? Is there some unforgiveness you haven't released from your heart? Is there an ex you can't get over? What about that mindset that tells you every man or woman is the same? Each of us has baggage in life that will weigh us down if we choose to hold on to it rather than cast it at the feet of Jesus through prayer and spending time in His presence.

We'll talk more about baggage later in our chapter on forgiveness, but let's start by opening the door to one important question: Have you thought of any habits in your life that you know God is chiseling away at? You know, those secret sins that no one is aware of except God (1 Samuel 16:7; Jeremiah 17:9–10)? It's unreasonable to believe that any of us would be perfect prior to marriage, but you must focus on developing some critical habits right now.

3. BUILD DISCIPLINES

Few of us would claim to be perfect, but it's possible that we are still blinded to some of the issues in our life that God wants to free us from. Let's dive into a few disciplines to form before your next relationship.

The Discipline of Communication

Assumptions are relationship killers. We can't expect others to read our minds. Healthy communication is essential in any relationship. I remember a time when, as happens in every marriage, something Safa said had me slightly offended. I honestly can't remember what exactly she said that made me frustrated with her, and that's because, honestly, it was trivial and I was simply being dramatic. The problem was, instead of addressing how I felt, I simply stayed bitter and uptight because "she should've known better." If she loved me, I should never have to worry about her saying something that I don't like, right? But me walking around with a vexed spirit didn't allow the peace of God to stay in the marriage. I was choosing to be immature in my demeanor toward her because I thought she should have known I was upset. The only problem was, Safa had no idea that I was offended by something she said. I was upset with her and wouldn't even tell her. Thankfully, she recognized my sulking, and I decided to finally express what was bothering me so we could work it out. Many of you may do the same thing I was guilty of: we avoid expressing ourselves and eventually cause a barrier of bitterness to harden. We think:

I shouldn't have to tell her that comment was rude; she should've known better.

I shouldn't have to tell him what I want for my birthday. If he loved me, he would definitely know.

If this person were who God had for me, I wouldn't have to tell them what I expect from them. God would show them.

All these assumptions we walk around with are harming our

relationships more than we realize. Imagine that you were dating someone and the two of you never clearly communicated that your goal was to wait until marriage for sex. If they made a pass at you, should you get upset? Of course. But if you're honest with yourself, it probably happened because the two of you had never discussed your values and intentions when it came to physical intimacy. Amos 3:3 asks this question: "Can two walk together, except they be agreed?" (KJV). When you vocalize how you feel and what you desire, the other person can get on the same page with you.

I have learned throughout the years that everyone likes to consider themselves "grown." Unfortunately, when people say that word, they are referring to their being old enough to do whatever they want without taking anyone's opinion or criticism into account. The thing is, all of us will age, but few of us will truly mature. We grow and mature when we begin to convey our feelings and emotions in a manner that isn't destructive but constructive. We voice how we feel and don't allow the one we're with to simply believe that all is well. Unspoken expectations will lead to unnecessary resentment. Our partner could've had an opportunity to change, but our feelings got in the way of them adjusting something that we didn't like. This may seem difficult for those of you who don't view yourself as confrontational, but if you choose to ignore how you feel, you can't get upset when they aren't able to meet the needs they didn't know you had.

It's always best to seek clarity before allowing assumptions to guide you. James 1:19 puts it this way: "Understand this, my dear brothers and sisters: You must all be quick to listen, slow to speak, and slow to get angry." It is best to be of one accord so the relationship can thrive, rather than face unnecessary conflict.

A lack of communication is at the root of many failed relationships, because you can't meet someone's expectations if they refuse to clearly communicate them. Instead of dropping hints and hoping for the best, be willing to be assertive and say what it is that you desire. Instead of assuming they should know when you're frustrated or allowing yourself to be infuriated when they're not meeting your expectations, tell them areas where they can improve. Be willing to be clear on what you find unacceptable or harmful. People only continue to treat us in a specific way if we tolerate it.

The Discipline of Service

Safa here. I want to jump in and tell you about something closely related to the assumptions and expectations Tovares has been talking about. I call it the "me mindset." And it's something we all need to ditch.

Instead of having a "me mindset," develop the discipline of embracing a servant's heart. Selfishness is possibly the most destructive and subtle habit each of us face. None of us would say that it's wrong to be happy. The problem arises when we believe our feelings and our expectations are more important than those of others.

You are in a relationship to serve the other person, not just to be served (also true in your relationships with your friends and family). Any relationship we have should glorify God, and it is vital to have a servant's heart if we are to do so. Now, that doesn't mean we shouldn't look forward to the benefits of that relationship, meaning what that person can do for us as well, but that should not be our focus.

Before I got married to Tovares, I must admit I was looking forward to what he could do for me a little more than what I could do for him. If you asked me why I wanted to get married, I might have said something like, "Well, because I'm looking for someone to grow old with. Someone who could protect me and make me feel like I'm the most beautiful girl in the world, someone who could give me children, someone who could give me a good massage after a long day of work." And what girl wouldn't want all these things? My whole life, even as a little girl, I knew I would one day want to get married to a Prince Charming who would sweep me off my feet! I had a Cinderella mentality that obscured my vision of what a real, godly relationship should be.

But after we got married, the closer I got to my husband and the closer I got to God, the more I realized my vision of relationships was blurred. God revealed to me that I was looking to receive more than to give, and that was why I wasn't truly satisfied. I quickly realized the more I sought to satisfy my husband's needs, the more I was satisfied myself. I was pleased to give to him in a capacity that represented the way God intended relationships to be. Now if you ask me why I am married to Tovares, other than the obvious purpose of glorifying God together, I would say, "I am married to this man to make him feel like he is the only man in the room, to give him beautiful children, to give him a massage after a long day's work, to make him feel special in whatever way I can." My focus has shifted, and my marriage has become one where I enjoy serving.

"Me, Myself and I" may be the title of a very influential song by the legendary artist Beyoncé, but it isn't the mentality to bring into a relationship. Marriage has taught us that "me" quickly becomes "we." The saying "happy wife, happy life" isn't the goal that God intended for marriage. We should actually be saying "happy spouse, happy house," because the goal should be to outdo each other in service (Romans 12:10). I don't think a godly relationship minimizes you and forces you to neglect your own desires, but the humility Christ desires us to walk in should always lead us to grow a heart for giving rather than receiving.

> We should actually be saying "happy spouse, happy house," because the goal should be to outdo each other in service.

The Discipline of Perseverance

We need to break the habit of quitting every time we are inconvenienced. It's quite astonishing how quickly we are willing to leave something before God tells us to. It's wonderful that society is making improvements in teaching people the value of self-care or valuing themselves, but has that led us to make a god out of comfort? If something doesn't fit how we feel, we are willing to walk away, even if it was the will of God for our lives.

I (Safa) have met many people who have jumped from church to church to find the "perfect" church for them. The problem with that is they'll be hopping around like the Easter Bunny until Jesus returns. The perfect church doesn't exist, because they're all made up of flawed human beings. God can be present in the church, but problems are inevitable once people are involved. I once left a church prematurely and God had to lead me back. The church hadn't changed, but God had planted me there for a reason; there were certain areas in my life He wanted to work on in that place. It's easy for us to find a more comfortable place, but we need to find where God desires us to be.

Some people jump from job to job because they feel undervalued, unappreciated, overworked, or simply stressed out. Almost 50 percent of millennials leave a job within a couple of years.[1] Culture will cheer them on for their bravery, but what if they should've stayed? I firmly believe the will of God isn't to force us into situations that are dangerous to our emotional, spiritual, or even physical health, but I do believe the will of God doesn't mean a life of ease. Sometimes God allows us to be in difficult situations so He can receive the glory, so souls can be won on the job, so we can develop patience, or because we are going to be the next leaders to change that broken environment. Serving Jesus doesn't excuse us from problems, but following Jesus does guarantee that God is present with us in our trouble (Psalm 46:1).

As Tovares mentioned, culture is conditioning our minds to think that if a relationship is no longer serving our needs, we should find someone else. My generation is very quick to brag on their "cut-off game." If you don't know what that means, it's a way of saying how quickly they will kick you out of their lives and have nothing to do with you. The problem with that is, that isn't the way God treats His children. If possible, instead of quitting on relationships, we should first aim to work through our differences and grow despite challenges with others (Romans 12:18). Conflict is never comfortable, but some of the best relationships are those where we can have difficult experiences and still love each other afterward, even if we agree to disagree.

The Discipline of Practicing Faithfulness

Many people desire a marriage relationship today but aren't willing to give up their single life. We must stop entertaining or pursuing multiple people if we desire to have a relationship that honors God. I (Tovares) can tell you that the fact that you are holding this book that Safa and I wrote together isn't a testament of how great our relationship has been, but it's proof of how faithful God really is. (You'll see why later on in our chapters on boundaries and forgiveness.) I realized that I never truly had the right boundaries in place prior to getting married. I was under the impression that if you're in a relationship, other people would automatically respect your relationship. However, seldom is that the case. Something about human nature causes us to desire things we shouldn't have. You don't believe me? Look at Adam and Eve in the garden of Eden. They had access to everything, but God said to not eat from one tree. The Enemy deceived Eve, and they disobeyed what God had planned (Genesis 3). Today, many of us break rules we know we shouldn't. If you have a driver's license, you may have been guilty of speeding. Underaged drinking is against the law, but many of us have done it. Let's not even mention the Ten Commandments, because we've all broken at least a few of them. But my point isn't to show you that we are guilty of sin; we all know that. My point is that due to our sinful human nature, we all tend to cross lines we shouldn't.

Some men desire a wife but still look at other women on social media or at the gym with lust. Some ladies desire a husband but are still entertaining six different guys in their inbox because their kindness is flattering. I've learned over time that the habits of faithfulness must be fixed prior to inviting someone into our lives romantically. I thought once I got married to a beautiful woman, my eyes would never drift again. But if you can't stop your eyes from wandering now, they won't stop when you're taken. Marriage has taught me that I need to develop a key component of the fruit of the Spirit: self-control (Galatians 5:22–23). If everyone who shows you a little attention or who gives a compliment is automatically stirring your emotions, that shows you may not be ready for a relationship. You don't want to date out of loneliness, but out of purpose. When you learn to not operate out of desperation while single, you'll know how to be rooted when in a relationship.

James 1:8 tells us, "A double minded man is unstable in all his ways" (KJV). This verse was written about the concept of seeking God in faith. But it applies to dating too. If you *waver* every time an opportunity arises, that shows an instability that isn't ready for a relationship. People will always show interest in you, but you shouldn't mishandle the heart of one of God's children. If you are pursuing marriage, which is a covenant between one man and one woman, you shouldn't allow your heart to *sway* between every person who catches your eye. If

I must pursue every woman who is attractive in my sight, like King Solomon in the Bible, I shouldn't be surprised when my lust for women turns my heart away from the Lord, as it did for him (1 Kings 11:4). People will tempt you when you're dating, so you must have a made-up mind not to sin before the opportunity arises.

When you get married and the minister instructs you to say "I do," you are inevitably saying *no* to everyone else. *No* to the other options that arise when your hormones are raging. *No* to the random guys sliding in your DMs when you're feeling lonely and insecure. *No* to the beautiful woman sending seductive images and heart eyes to your pictures. Obviously, marriage is different from dating, but we shouldn't practice reckless dating. Try to be intentional now while in the dating stage so you are prepared to commit. We should make our intentions known to the person we are with. Both parties should be aware that the goal is to pursue marriage and that neither is entertaining multiple people on the side. It's careless to approach a relationship without the desire for marriage, because we end up investing our emotions, and hearts get broken.

Embrace Financial Discipline

In the past whenever I (Safa) saw a couple get divorced, I always speculated that some form of infidelity or abuse took place in the relationship. Not to be judgmental, but I assumed those would have to be the only reasons a couple could go from being "in love" to deciding to separate. However, one of the most common reasons for divorce is conflicts over money.[2] That's right—finances have destroyed many relationships, possibly because of one person being too reckless, or overly possessive of it, or simply not making enough, which causes a strain on the marriage. That's why poor spending habits must be addressed as early as possible. Before you even being dating, learn the importance of financial stewardship and creating a budget. John Maxwell once said, "A budget is telling your money where to go instead of wondering where it went."3 You don't want to go into marriage without knowing you can tell your money where to go.

I had a large amount of student loan debt going into marriage. More than I realized. That didn't mean I wasn't ready for marriage, but it did show me I had to make adjustments so it wouldn't affect the future that I was praying for. I don't claim to be an expert on finances, but I do know that gaining more money shouldn't be the main goal of life. Our focus should be to properly steward what God places in our hands. If we can't properly steward $10, it doesn't make sense that we ask God to bless us with $1,000. The Bible makes it clear to us that those who are faithful with little can be trusted to be faithful with much (Matthew 25:23).

Culture places a large emphasis on material things that matter little in the grand scheme of life. A big house or nice car doesn't help when your relationship is crumbling. Neither does a brand-new outfit if we have no money to invest in our family's future or to give to help others. We all must learn to budget and be responsible prior to marriage so our future relationship won't suffer due to our desire to appear "rich."

FOCUS ON JESUS FIRST

I (Tovares) can tell you that all these disciplines depend on one important thing: to love someone else properly, you must first love Jesus. If a person isn't committed to Jesus, they may commit to you, but they will never show you the unconditional love God intended. Now, I know that's a bold statement that many of you will disagree with, but it is a fact. God is love (1 John 4:8). How can you love without Him? You can't. The church is seeing a rise in divorce because of a constant decline in our love for God, our obedience to His Word, and our willingness to forgive as Christ has forgiven us. An unsaved person may be kind, but they can never truly exude the fruit of the Spirit on a consistent basis within a marriage—especially when the storms come.

When we're seeking marriage, we all must work to end bad habits and form new ones, but we must understand that the true reasoning behind all this is to please God, not simply to get something from Him. Our obedience does lead to blessings, but that isn't why we obey. We obey God because it honors Him; and as we obey Him, we know that He is preparing us for the plans that He has in store for us (Jeremiah 29:11). While we may not know what all to expect in preparation for marriage, we can plan accordingly—just like I learned to do when trying to make lasagna for Safa that first disastrous time. We can get all our ingredients, equipment, pots, pans, and seasonings ready rather than just showing up in the kitchen and experiencing problems like I did. These days, I try to stock up on more ingredients than

I need to ensure there are no issues when I tell Safa I'm making lasagna. It can't hurt to go the extra mile when you are getting ready for marriage either. While you wait, be sure to prepare for what you are praying for.

2

A FOUNDATION FOR TRUE LOVE

I (Safa) love to build things. I find it therapeutic.
I love putting things together and seeing the stability that comes
from random pieces forming one unit that can hold the weight of
whatever I want to place on top of it. Maybe that's why one of my
favorite games to play is Jenga. If you haven't played that before,
it's a game with building blocks where you constantly remove
blocks from the bottom of a tower and place them at the top,
but you must be careful to not let any fall. The difficulty of the
game arises as the foundational pieces are removed. Eventually
the tower won't be able to stand due to holes all around the infrastructure. The key is to always keep the foundation solid. To be
honest, I find Jenga similar to dating. The tower, or relationship
in this case, can stand as long as the foundation is right, but
things begin to crumble when the groundwork isn't resolute.

If I were to ask any woman I met today, "What are you looking for in a man?" chances are every last one of us would agree on at least one thing: stability. Sure, we desire attractive husbands. Strong men to help protect us and the children. Men who are faithful, kind, and generous. If we ask that same question to the men—"What are you looking for in a woman?"—you may hear the same answers. Some men might say they're looking for a woman who is supportive or nurturing. Society tells us to focus on these traits when we plan to settle down. We might even think we've hit the jackpot simply because someone is romantic, faithful, and has a good sense of humor. All of these attributes are great, but they are really added layers to the person. Someone's sense of humor alone isn't going to sustain a relationship that honors God. Nothing is funny if God isn't pleased. Their earning potential is of little importance if that's the foundation. Money can't help us in the face of infidelity, abuse, or dishonor. Their beauty or their body won't be impressive when you see they won't help you cook or clean, or communicate in times of conflict.

So what is a solid foundation in a mate? I like to think of building a relationship in similar fashion to the process in creating a building. In the construction industry, you might hear the term *compound defects*. That means that when you're establishing the first set of building blocks or preparing the ground for the infrastructure of your building, if you don't have a solid foundation, the rest of the building will progressively break down. One could have the best-looking layers to the most glorious building, and yet that lofty building is doomed to fail if the foundation wasn't properly secured. You could have purchased the most awe-inspiring home in the entire city, but if the foundation of your home isn't stable, you are bound to have issues and become best friends with your insurance company. From the outside looking in, marvelous architecture may turn heads, but it is the foundation that allows it to stand and be admirable and worthy of praise. The human eye pays attention to what's on the outside, but the builder knows that one must first have the right foundation.

When it comes to dating, many of us have been enticed by the beauty of someone on our arms. It feels good to have the "arm candy" or a "knight in shining armor" who we want to bring out in public with us. We enjoy getting our "likes" up on social media with this amazing person. We want to show everyone a man or woman we can start a future with—build generational wealth, raise a family, travel the world, and enjoy one another's company. In our pursuit of these things, many of us have overlooked the most important aspect of a person: the foundation. We've found ourselves creating relationships that God isn't a part of, and then trying to add Him to the picture later. In Matthew 7:24–25, Jesus said, "Anyone who listens to my teaching and follows it is wise, like a person who builds a house on solid rock. Though the rain comes in torrents and the floodwaters rise and the winds beat against that house, it won't collapse because it is built on bedrock." His teaching shows us that problems arise in all of our lives, but those who have Him as their foundation can endure hard times. Starting relationships with a foundation of lust never truly helps us have the relationship God intended for us. Hebrews 13:4 says that marriage is honorable and should be pure, and that is what happens when a couple keeps Jesus as the center of their relationship.

Many people believe that most marriages end in divorce because people simply "fall out of love." I don't believe that's always the case. Perhaps some of these relationships didn't become bad or lose love along the way, but their foundations were broken from the outset. The starting point showed them many red flags of spiritual instability, but they decided to overlook them and hope they would fade away. Unfortunately, red flags don't change colors over time alone. Unresolved, unaddressed problems from the outset will turn into the very things that cause the building we are forming to deteriorate. It's just like the construction concept of compound defects. We must ensure that we build a solid foundation in the relationships we create, because our connections are destined for failure if we are building on faulty ground.

In Philippians 4:1, we see Paul admonishing the church to stand firm in their faith. Paul knew that it wasn't enough to say we love God, but we had to be rooted in Christ. Spiritual instability has become an epidemic, because it has become more popular to call ourselves Christian than to actually follow Christ. Paul had to correct the church in Galatia because they were being led astray by the wrong influences (Galatians 1:6–10). He told them that anyone who would come and teach them a new gospel that didn't save them would be accursed, even if the message came from an angel. The church must be aware that some people may seem to benefit our lives, but their motives aren't pure. In the same way, in some relationships the person you're attracted to may seem like an angel, but their purpose is to stop you from being rooted in Christ.

Still not convinced of the value of a good foundation? One of the most famous structural mistakes is seen in the Leaning Tower of Pisa located in Pisa, Italy. This attraction is something people actually travel to Italy to see, but it was never the intention of the builder for the tower to lean in such a manner. Before creating this tower to house the bell of the Pisa Cathedral complex, they didn't notice the foundation wasn't as balanced and durable as expected. The tower began to lean during construction.

In 1981, a construction error at the Hyatt Regency Hotel in Kansas City, Missouri, caused devastating losses. The hotel had been built with a "minor" design flaw in its skybridges (elevated walkways above its atrium). The hotel was beautiful and elaborate, but builders didn't notice that some of their hanger rods were bearing excessive pressure from the bridges floating above the hotel lobby. When two of the bridges collapsed, 114 people were killed and another 216 were injured.[1] The groundwork may seem the most insignificant to some, but it determines whether a structure stands or falls. This is why, as believers, we must understand the importance of dating, and eventually marrying, someone who shares our faith.

EQUALLY YOKED

When I (Tovares) was growing up, the spiritual leaders in my life emphasized the importance of not dating unbelievers. I understand now why they would consistently highlight that, especially after all the terrible mistakes I made ignoring them in my efforts to be "cool." The apostle Paul said that we shouldn't be unequally yoked together with unbelievers (2 Corinthians 6:14). A righteous person shouldn't be yoked together with an unrighteous person. When the Bible references a yoke, it's not talking about the egg yolk you had for breakfast. Paul was alluding to a couple things found in the Law and in the farming practices of the day. Deuteronomy 22:10 said not to allow an ox and a donkey to plow together. A yoke was typically a wooden crosspiece used to fasten the necks of two animals. Farmers would attach it to a plow or cart, and it would allow the animals to share the load, rather than one animal doing all the work while the other didn't pull its weight. For the yoke to be effective, the animals would have to be somewhat close in size for the cart to pull evenly.

Paul used this illustration because many understood the principles of farming, but they might not have grasped the concept in their relationships. Once someone is in Christ, they become a new creation (2 Corinthians 5:17). When this takes place, God washes our pasts away and begins to do a new work within us called *sanctification*. That is just a fancy way of saying God is purifying us and making us holy and more like Him. A person with a heart for Christ should no longer have the same desires and interests as someone who isn't serving God. That's why when Paul said not to yoke together with an unbeliever, he didn't specify which unbeliever is the type of sinner to avoid. Many of us have mastered the art of labeling the "big or little" sins. Some think that God is in heaven picking which sinner He wants to love and those He hates. I've seen many quick to condemn someone who steals, but they are quiet on the unforgiveness and hatred in their heart. Or we can condemn the person for fornication, but do so while being guilty of envy and jealousy.

When Paul taught us about not yoking together with unbelievers, he was implying that as believers, we have a calling from God that is hard to fulfill when we connect to the wrong company. It's not that you shouldn't befriend them. Kindness and friendship-building are possibly the best ways to share the gospel with anyone. The issue comes when we form an intimate connection with someone who isn't spiritually stable enough for a relationship yet. Not that every unbeliever is automatically scandalous and vulgar, but we need a firm foundation to stand on when it comes to forging biblical relationships. It's not possible for someone you're dating to lead you closer to Christ if they aren't first aware of who He is. It's absurd of me to think that my wife should submit to me as a husband if I'm not first submitted to Christ (Ephesians 5:22–24).

Christians live to honor and bring glory to God (1 Corinthians 10:31)—or we should at least strive to. Someone who isn't following Jesus won't have a desire to live a life of obedience to Him and denial of their flesh. They may respect your walk with God, but they should be willing to offer a helping hand in that process. I once dated an unbeliever and thought it was perfectly fine because she never criticized me for being a Christian. But she never cared to seek God with me, attend services, or even read a Christian book. I should have known that just because she tolerated my walk with God didn't mean that she valued my spiritual growth. God desires for us to find someone with the same kingdom mindset so our relationship, which should be a blessing, won't turn into a spiritual burden that limits our relationship with Jesus. My wife has shown me that it is a great benefit to have someone at your side who isn't solely attending service with you, but is helping you pursue the heart of God.

Paul says it like this in 2 Corinthians 6:16–18:

What union can there be between God's temple and idols? For we are the temple of the living God. As God said:

"I will live in them
    and walk among them.
I will be their God,
    and they will be my people.
Therefore, come out from among unbelievers,
    and separate yourselves from them, says
        the LORD.
Don't touch their filthy things,
    and I will welcome you.
And I will be your Father,
    and you will be my sons and daughters,
        says the LORD Almighty."

God makes it clear that there is no reason for believers to create these relationships with unbelievers, because the temple of God should be consecrated from worldly influences. Surely some people have dated someone who was an unbeliever and eventually that person changed and found God, but those are exceptions, not the standard. God's desire isn't for us to simply hope that they change, but to first see spiritual fruit being produced. Because a relationship without God at the center will eventually lead to a downfall at some point.

Other than the fact that the Bible says to avoid binding together with an unbeliever, these unequally yoked relationships can have more lasting effects than we realize. One of the biggest reasons we should steer clear of these "situationships" is that they can't edify you spiritually if they aren't first submitted to the Holy Spirit. I (Tovares) have dated unsaved women whom I could bond with in certain areas, but I couldn't lean on them when it came to the things of God. They wouldn't tell me that I need to drop my faith to be with them, but they also couldn't strengthen my spirit when I felt burdened or spiritually exhausted. It's like trying to rescue someone who is drowning in a pool. Unless they surrender, their fighting and panic can actually drown both parties unintentionally. On the flip side, if both parties are able to swim, you don't have to worry about them harming themselves or you as you get closer to them. When it comes to dating, it isn't our duty to save the other person. Salvation belongs to God, and we must allow Him to do the work before we form the relationship.

If we are brutally honest, unbelievers can be nicer than some people you meet in your local church. It's easy for us to say that who we date shouldn't even matter if Christians are causing the same problems, if not more, than unbelievers. But the truth is they can't help point you to the source of true joy if they haven't experienced Jesus for themselves. Being connected to the wrong person can harm you over time. Samson was still greatly used by God, but his relationships led to him breaking his Nazirite covenant (Numbers 6). In Judges 3, the Bible says the children of Israel were around some ungodly nations—Canaanites, Hittites, Amorites, and more. Due to them mingling with those people, the Bible says they began to serve their gods as well (v. 6). As believers we must understand that who we choose to date and eventually marry will affect our worship. Psalm 106:35 says, "But [they] were mingled among the heathen, and learned their works" (KJV). We may think we have it under control, but it is easier to become lukewarm than we realize. God promised to be our Father and welcome us, but He also told the church in Corinth through Paul that they had to separate themselves from unequally yoked relationships first (2 Corinthians 6:16–18).

Despite many of us understanding that we shouldn't marry an unbeliever, I wonder how many of us understand that we can still be in a spiritually unstable commitment with someone who is a Christian. Yes, they may be saved, but there's more to being a godly spouse than simply being a Christian. God wants us to focus more on fruit than church attendance. Often, we ask God to provide a godly spouse, but we get frustrated with His timing. If we don't see Mr. Right in our inbox by next week, we are just going to date the first guy from church who compliments us, even though he may be lukewarm. We are tired of waiting on a woman who exemplifies the virtuous woman in Proverbs 31, so we are willing to take the Proverbs 5 woman whom Solomon warned against. In Proverbs 31, we read about the woman who is admirable in every way, but chapter 5 tells us about someone who may seem attractive and desirable, but the outcome leads to destruction. To ensure that we have marriages that glorify God, we must place Him as our foundation. Both parties have to do more than believe Jesus is their Savior; they must view Jesus as their Lord. You want someone who did more than say a sinner's prayer—someone filled and led by the Holy Spirit in their heart and mind. Someone who allows God to guide them and direct their path. Someone who follows and trusts in His Word rather than being led by urges and hormones. We must seek to create a relationship yielded to His purpose, because only then will we find true joy. Before Safa took me seriously in my pursuit for her heart, she needed to be sure my life exemplified some form of stability. It would be unwise for her to see me acting carnally and worldly and still expect me to lead a godly home. The very first thing we must notice in a potential spouse, or even a close friend, is whether they are connected to Jesus.

In 1 Corinthians 5:9–13, Paul put it this way:

> When I wrote to you before, I told you not to associate with people who indulge in sexual sin. But I wasn't talking about unbelievers who indulge in sexual sin, or are greedy, or cheat people, or worship idols. You would have to leave this world to avoid people like that. I meant that you are not to associate with anyone who claims to be a believer yet indulges in sexual sin, or is greedy, or worships idols, or is abusive, or is a drunkard, or cheats people. Don't even eat with such people.
>
> It isn't my responsibility to judge outsiders, but it certainly

is your responsibility to judge those inside the church who are sinning. God will judge those on the outside; but as the Scriptures say, "You must remove the evil person from among you."

Reading that scripture for the first time was honestly alarming for me. Why would Paul tell us to avoid anyone? Kicking someone out of church wasn't something I would ever expect to be recommended by someone spiritual. But Paul understood something that many of us fail to grasp. Galatians 5:9 says, "A little leaven leaveneth the whole lump" (KJV). Meaning that it only takes a little bit of yeast to affect the entire batch of dough. A little bit of carnality is all it takes for a spiritual person to begin to compromise and drift away from their desire to grow. A relationship that is only partly stable won't last over time. A chair missing a leg will eventually wobble and fall, no matter how beautiful the chair is. Paul was telling the church in Corinth that it's understandable when unbelievers decide to abide in sinful commitments, but those who consider themselves to be believers must avoid people bringing them back to the place that God delivered them out of. Being married to a godly woman has been a consistent reminder for me that I can grow deeper into who God called me to be. While I aim to *constantly* encourage her to be who God has called her to be without fear or reservation, she does that for me and more. Those are aspects I would not experience with someone in an unsaved or lukewarm lifestyle.

Being a Christian means your life revolves around Jesus. If someone believes they can date someone simply because they claim to believe in Jesus, it's like believing someone is clean because they have purchased soap. Don't just look for someone who goes to church, but see how they surrender to Jesus and how they uplift you in your walk with Him. That's where the journey actually begins.

WHAT MAKES A GOOD FOUNDATION?

Before Safa and I began courting, we were friends for a few years. When I began seeking God regarding a spouse, I ran into plenty of women I didn't get God's approval for. I saw women with beauty who didn't have the character that I was looking for. I met ladies with moral character lacking in maturity in their spiritual life. I knew I had to find a woman who offered more than her beauty, because looks aren't enough to help us reach our purpose. Safa and I tried to date a couple years after high school, but it didn't go as planned. I ended it in an immature manner, and it's only by God's grace that we were able to remain friends. Thankfully, God protected her from my immaturity. A few years later, I began praying for God's direction, because I knew Safa was the woman who didn't simply capture my eyes but had a solid walk with Jesus outside of me. I knew I desired a relationship with her, because she was the woman who could show me an image of what Proverbs 31 describes.

Proverbs 31 speaks about a woman who is of noble character, is a hard worker in her home and community, is generous, is loving, and fears the Lord. Before I met my wife, beauty was all

I believed to be necessary to have a healthy and holy marriage. But the Bible and my wife have shown me that who you connect to truly matters. Being equally yoked allows you to have a spouse who helps you face any storm and trust in God no matter the season.

Many times I wrongly thought I could overlook the fact that someone I was dating wasn't firm in their spiritual life. They'd be my "project," and I'd help guide them and develop them into someone who served Jesus. I have overlooked character flaws because I thought they'd plan to develop a walk with Jesus later. But people are not our projects. They must desire to know Jesus for themselves, not so they can be with you. Have you ever been there? It's an admirable approach in some ways, but it isn't healthy, and it can be very draining. God wants you in a relationship that honors Him, not one where you have to beg and plead for the other person to pray or study. Not one where you know they'll want to spend time with you, but you question whether they are producing spiritual fruit. Not one where they are romantic for date night, but they'll treat attending church services like they're going to the dentist to get teeth pulled.

As we've mentioned before, the Bible says that if a person is double minded, all their ways will be unstable (James 1:6–8). Meaning, they can be attractive, but if their heart is wavering spiritually, we should expect to see inconsistencies in every aspect of their life. God wants all of us to grow spiritually, and that occurs through disciplines like prayer, fasting, and studying God's Word. If we are only choosing to seek God when we feel like it, chances are we will limit our growth. If we only exercised when we felt like it, none of us would get into shape. Just because the person you want to date is beautiful or handsome doesn't mean you can overlook an inconsistent walk with God.

When laying the foundation of your relationship, you both must have a foundation that is rooted in Christ. If Jesus is the foundation only on Sundays, you can expect a marriage that only considers God when it's convenient or when you're around other believers. If Jesus is truly both of your hearts' desire, though, you can expect a marriage that helps both of you serve Him. A marriage with the right foundation allows a relationship with a biblical focus—a kingdom mindset.

RISKY CONNECTIONS

When God has a plan for your life, you can't just connect to any random person. You have to be intentional with who you choose. Not because you're better than anyone else, but you know that person will affect your walk with God. Our relationships should guide us closer to God rather than further away from Him. Other than Jesus, Solomon is known to be the wisest man to ever live. He had wisdom to rule God's people and give them instructions (Proverbs) that we still follow to this day. Despite all his wisdom, he entertained relationships that weren't anchored in a godly foundation. He knew who the true God was, but his wives didn't. The Bible mentions him associated with "strange women," meaning they were foreigners and didn't worship the same God as Solomon (1 Kings 11:1 KJV). With his relationship choices, he married according to the flesh instead of the Spirit. He chose women who could make him feel good rather than help him do what God had called him to do. First Kings 11:4–6 says, "In Solomon's old age, they turned his heart to worship other gods instead of being completely faithful to the LORD his God, as his father, David, had been. Solomon worshiped Ashtoreth, the goddess of the Sidonians, and Molech, the detestable god of the Ammonites. In this way, Solomon did what was evil in the LORD's sight; he refused to follow the LORD completely, as his father, David, had done."

At the end of Solomon's life, he lost his way spiritually. He was warned that marrying foreign women would shift the trajectory of his walk with God, but his desires led him rather than the Holy Spirit (vv. 2–3). He began to drift due to his connections with these ungodly women. Solomon started off his journey of leadership asking God for wisdom (1 Kings 3), but he allowed that same wisdom to slip as time progressed. That's the issue we face when we form fleshly connections rather than kingdom-minded partnerships. This same scenario can happen to the godly ladies out there. Connecting to men who aren't serving Jesus can lead to the same outcome Solomon experienced. Many of us trust God in every aspect of life except the romantic. We must know that even though we may have pure intentions, the relationship must still have a consecrated focus if we are to get closer to Jesus instead of sin.

It is God's will for us all to have a kingdom-focused mindset. In Matthew 6:33, Jesus said, "Seek ye first the kingdom of

God, and his righteousness; and all these things shall be added unto you" (KJV). When Jesus spoke this to His disciples, I'm well aware He wasn't referring to their dating life. Jesus was more concerned with changing them in the time He had with them, rather than changing their relationship status. But He taught them a principle they needed to understand about God. When you seek His kingdom first above all things, you don't have to worry about Him providing for you in other areas. Many of us have aimed to achieve this principle in reverse. We have pursued the relationships, jobs, happiness, freedom, and so many other things we want, but we went after them before seeking Jesus. When we aim to grasp God's blessings without seeking God's direction or His approval, we end up with distractions from His plan for our life. God desires you to pursue Him first and allow Him to guide your steps, because He will lead us down the right path (Proverbs 3:5–6).

Our culture says it doesn't matter if the one you're with loves Jesus or not; as long as you're happy, that's all that matters. It says, "Love is love, so follow your heart." But the Word of God warns us of following our emotions, because we all have hearts that will deceive us and emotions that could cause us to go in the wrong direction (Jeremiah 17:9). Instead of following what makes us happy, we should pursue what makes us holy. A Christ-centered union is what God desires for us. He wants us in a relationship where we can help one another get closer to our goals and to God. If we make the mistake of marrying someone who isn't helping us spiritually, we will begin to adopt some of their habits and worship the same idols they have in their life (Psalm

Instead of
following
what makes
us happy, we
should pursue
what makes
us holy.

106:35–36). Who you marry will affect who you worship. When your relationship is kingdom-minded, your partner will help you worship Jesus above all else. Godly marriages aren't accidental. It takes two parties in a passionate pursuit of Christ for us to not lose our way spiritually.

When aiming to maintain a relationship that honors God, we need to look to Christ, not our culture. Jesus has shown us a consistent love that desires the best for us. When we walk in His love, He prepares us to have a good future.

WHAT GROUND ARE YOU STANDING ON?

While it's easy to spot flaws in someone else's character, we must also do the arduous work of examining ourselves. When Jesus taught His Sermon on the Mount, He had to emphasize the fact that we shouldn't expect to take the small splinter out of our neighbor's eye if we aren't taking the beam out of our own eye first (Matthew 7:4–5). If we want to have a spiritually stable relationship, we must ensure that we are not unstable in our lives. If we choose to remain unstable in our Christian journey—and, yes, it is a choice—we will surely be loved by God, but we will be inviting others into our dysfunction. It's saying, "That's just how I am," instead of committing to work on becoming who God has called us to be. Now is the time to prepare for what we are praying for. It's dangerous for God's greatest treasures, His children, to be entrusted to and knitted into the lives of people who won't lead them closer to Him.

When Jesus taught the parable about building on a rock, He showed us that the foundation is everything. When you are tempted to build a relationship on something that isn't Him, remember what Safa told you about the Hyatt Regency collapse. Remember what happens in Jenga. An unstable foundation will cause a fall, no matter how beautiful things appear on the outside. Desiring marriage is a great thing, but we must ensure that both parties have a connection to God that is solid enough to withstand storms. It's harder for a believer with a mind made up to love Jesus to stumble into sin than it is for someone who is simply casual in their Christianity. Be rooted and grounded in His Word, and seek His truth and His presence before seeking a spouse. We must commit to having the right resolve prior to getting into a relationship.

WHO'S ON YOUR TEAM?

When I (Tovares) was in high school, I played football for arguably the strictest coach there was. Coach Frazier built a name for himself by turning boys into men and weak teenagers into great football players. I was literally the weakest player on the team when I tried out in my freshman year. Coach Frazier made us repeat a saying every single time we crossed the track and stepped onto the football field: "I will not let my teammates down." Whether it was for practice or a game, whether we won or lost the match or maybe were just running off to get a quick bathroom break, we'd say, "I will not let my teammates down" every time we entered the field. At the time, it felt pointless and a little outdated of him to demand that from us teenagers, but there was a lesson behind it. Coach Frazier taught us that every time we had the opportunity to play the game we loved, we weren't solely doing it for ourselves. We were competing for and with each other. Even if I didn't like the person lined up next to me in the locker room, when we got on the field, we were one unit. There isn't an *i* in *team*, so there wouldn't be any of us forgetting that we had to be there for our brothers. Safa played flag football at her high school and can also attest that her coach drove home the point of working together.

Saying "I will not let my teammates down" may seem like an insignificant practice, but it made a difference. There was a battle on the field that we were committed to fighting alongside one another. If I missed my on-field assignment, someone else would be compromised or have to do extra, unnecessary work. A lackadaisical approach to the game could get myself or others hurt. How much more necessary is it for us to be there for our brothers and sisters in Christ, as we are in a serious battle? The fact is, a daily battle is being fought our souls, and we have an Enemy who aims to knock us off track spiritually (1 Peter 2:11). Society tells us that our lifestyle is our business, but sometimes we need to remind ourselves that our goal is to help others grow into who God created them to be as well. First Corinthians 12 informs us that we all make up the body of Christ, so it is imperative that we connect to the right community if we are to live the lives God intended for us.

SELF-MADE CHRISTIANS

When God was creating our world, the Bible constantly mentions that the process was "good." The light, the land and seas, the vegetation—all "good." When God saw fit to make humanity, He decided to make us in His image and likeness (Genesis 1:26–27). After making all these things, God reflected on His work and said to Himself that it was "very good!" (1:31).

As time progressed with Adam in the garden with the animals, God thought to Himself that there was an issue. He finally saw something that wasn't good. Remember what that was? It was Adam being alone (Genesis 2:18). This story always fascinates me. I'm coming back to it again to emphasize a particular point: we often overlook the fact that Adam was never alone. He had the animals and he had God. Technically, if we have God, we should have everything that we need. Right? Well, not necessarily. You see, *God created us for community*. Many times, people use this verse to justify why every person is *expected* to be married, but that isn't the principle God is showing us here. God is teaching us that we aren't supposed to do life alone, whether that refers to our relationship status or our friendships. Many people think they can have a thriving relationship with God without His people, but that isn't what God desires for us. He knows it's better to have two instead of one (Ecclesiastes 4:9–12). He also wants us to understand that who we connect to is more important than how many people we connect to, because the wrong connections can destroy our lives if they are influencing us away from Jesus: "Bad company corrupts good character" (1 Corinthians 15:33). A few godly friends are much more valuable than being surrounded by people distracting you from your purpose.

Society constantly pushes us to be self-reliant. Countless actors and rappers remind you they "made it out the trenches" or the streets. Thousands, if not millions, of self-help books try to convince you that you can make it out of debt and live your best life because the power is already within you. Safa even went shopping for a planner once and noticed that one of the "inspiring" terms printed on the inside was *self-made*. All these things may not be bad or sinful, but they do tend to convince us that we can do things alone. Unfortunately for us, none of us can make it on our own. Neither can we live in a manner that pleases God if we decide to do our own thing instead of doing it His way. We may gain everything our hearts have ever desired, but the process could have been easier and more rewarding if we'd had help.

The reality is that we can't do this Christian walk on our own (Hebrews 10:25). Think about it: we don't need to go to the gym and eat healthy to be alive, but those are key components essential to a healthy lifestyle. We don't need to get our oil changed in our car, but that car surely won't work forever without getting those maintenance checks. We don't have to go to work when we don't feel like it, but we still show up because there wouldn't be a check waiting for us if we stayed home. There are many things that we may not *have* to do as Christians, but they are beneficial for what God has planned for us. When God saw Adam without a companion of his own, He saw something that wasn't good. It isn't the will of God for you to be out on your own either.

WHAT IS BIBLICAL ACCOUNTABILITY?

Growing up, I had a bad taste in my mouth when it came to the idea of being accountable to a community. It seemed like another way for the church to control my every move or criticize every decision that I made. If I wanted to go somewhere, I needed to get "permission." Even when I was older, it seemed like I wasn't allowed to think for myself. I avoided listening to others because I thought it was just another way for them to supervise me. As I matured, though, I realized that accountability was necessary for many reasons. In Luke 12:48, Jesus said, "to whom much is given, much will be required" (BLB). When God entrusts us with His Spirit on the inside and in various roles in our lives, we are expected to maintain a certain standard. In Titus 1, Paul showed us that certain leaders are held to a different standard than others in the church, and we see all throughout Scripture that God aims to bring a separation between His children and the world. Accountability also connects us to the body of Christ. If God allows us to be connected to others, there are certain expectations we should desire to abide by.

Take Paul holding Peter accountable for the division that was occurring in Galatians 2, for example. Peter was still engaging in practices that separated Jewish from Gentile believers, even though they were supposed to be acting as one community. So Paul spoke up and let him know that wasn't right. Without Paul, a dangerous division could have taken hold in the early church. That's how God leads us and benefits us through accountability.

To truly understand why accountability is essential, we must bust any myths we may believe regarding this necessary tool. Accountability isn't a way to tell you how sinful you are. This isn't some person in a suit informing you that you fell into sin and God is ready to send you to hell. This isn't an older woman in the church telling you that you can't marry someone without her first giving you the green light. Being accountable is simply taking responsibility for our actions. All human relationships need accountability, because we are all sinful without the grace of God. A president who answers to no one can become a dictator or abusive with their power. A pastor who isn't accountable to anyone might create a church that exists to praise and obey them rather than God. A store manager who isn't accountable to anyone may steal all the inventory. An employee who isn't accountable to anyone can show up to work simply when they feel like it. We all know it's important to be liable to someone, but many of us avoid this when it comes to church. However, Christian liberty doesn't exempt us from listening to our brothers and sisters in Christ who care for us.

As believers, we are all supposed to give an account for our actions. And judgment day shouldn't be the only time we answer for them. In 1 Corinthians 5, Paul addressed the immorality that was beginning to take root in the church. It had gotten bad enough for him to say that a person needed to be removed from the community due to their actions (v. 13). It's essential for us all to submit to leaders and have godly peers around us who can help us become who God destined us to be. To be frank, I would rather my church family tell me that I am making mistakes so I can fix them instead of God having to judge the actions I could have adjusted.

Growing up in church, I (Safa) always had a form of accountability from leaders as well as my peers. I remember updating my profile photo on one social media account to one that was slightly provocative in order to grab the attention of a guy I had a crush on. At the time, I didn't see the dangers in it. I just saw the reward, which was getting him to notice me as hopefully more than just a friend. I was about fourteen at the time, and one of my close friends saw this and immediately advised me to reconsider what I was doing and remove the photo. She first let me know that she cared way too much about me to watch me fall, then she opened my eyes to not only how dangerous my actions could be but also how poorly they represented the young lady God was molding me into.

I believe having accountability at such a tender point in my adolescent youth steered me from going down many broad roads to destruction, more so now in my adult years when many of my decisions weigh heavier, because I have more at stake. I have my personal relationship with Christ, my family, and my ministry, all of which I have worked very hard to maintain. What I do affects more than just me, and I cannot afford to not have accountability. The same goes for you; as Christians, our actions not only affect us but the body of Christ as a whole.

Culture tells our youth that they don't need to answer to anyone—that our actions should be left up to individual judgment without restriction. Unfortunately, that only leads to sin, and it simply contradicts the Bible. Samson was a man who was clearly anointed by God, but due to his poor judgment, he ended up in relationships and fighting battles he probably could have avoided (Judges 13–16). Proverbs 11:14 informs us that "Where no counsel is, the people fall: but in the multitude of counsellors, there is safety" (KJV). The Bible must be our guide, and God allows people in our lives to help steer us closer to Jesus and away from destructive decisions. Some relationships allow us to be more vulnerable than others, but we must understand that transparency with the people God wants in our lives will help us find healing and strength (James 5:16). Our fears try to tell us that others will judge us and ostracize us, but the right accountability partner will strengthen and help restore us. Now, don't walk away with the impression that you need to start telling your deepest, darkest secrets to every person in your church. To be honest, some things don't need to be brought up at all unless you bring them to God in prayer.

Finding the right people can be scary, but we should focus on the reward. Staying isolated might not be in our best interests, but godly community is both edifying and a blessing. We have to exercise discernment in who we are vulnerable with. We must love everyone, but that doesn't mean we can trust everyone to be in our inner circles. I have learned that the ladies God placed in my life helped me become who God wants me to be. So let's dive a little deeper into those we have in close proximity to us.

SO, WHO'S IN YOUR CIRCLE?

The most common question that comes up when you talk about accountability is simply, "Who should I be accountable to?" It really matters who we allow to speak truth and wisdom into our lives. And surrounding ourselves with the wrong people can be dangerous! Let us tell you a story from the Bible that may shed some light on that. In 2 Samuel 13, Amnon had an ungodly obsession with his sister Tamar. He was wise enough to know he shouldn't have her, but that didn't stop him from desiring to be with her. Eventually his demeanor appeared dejected enough for others to notice. There is a possibility he wasn't going to act on his impulses, but his friend Jonadab encouraged him to take advantage of her. We won't get into much detail here, because we will dive into that more in our chapter on boundaries. But suffice it to say that Amnon lost his life, and Tamar's life was destroyed because Amnon listened to the wrong friend. Proverbs 13:20 tells us, "Walk with the wise and become wise; associate with fools and get in trouble." No matter how much time you spend together or how much the wrong friend cares for you, the wrong voices in your ear can be devastating to your future. Our associations can determine our future.

Finding godly friends isn't an easy task, but it is a choice we are to strive for daily. We need that kind of support if we are going to pursue a healthy dating relationship with someone. Biblical accountability helps us treat the person we are with in a godly manner and allows those around us to build us up. Amnon's and Tamar's lives were destroyed not just because of Amnon's actions but also because of his associations. So we feel inclined to ask: Who are you listening to? Who is in your circle? Are you accountable to people who desire greatness from you, or are you being led astray because of a Jonadab—the type of person who is close to you but isn't pointing you toward Jesus? Or are you listening to friends who are causing you to turn away from biblical convictions?

WE ALL NEED SOMEONE TO
TELL US THE TRUTH

I (Tovares) battled with lust for years. At some points, I just figured that is just the way I was and God would never forgive me. I knew what the Bible said, but I couldn't find my way into actually living what I was reading or hearing from the pulpit. Eventually, I felt the urge to ask God to surround me with more godly men. It didn't happen overnight, but gradually I attained more friends who desired to push me further into my purpose. Now, let me preface this by saying that it wasn't solely friends who made me decide to start crucifying my fleshly desires. All of us who claim to be Christians should be striving for this standard (Galatians 5:24). But I can honestly say that a godly friend is one of the greatest benefits someone can have, not just in overcoming lust, but in pursuing righteousness. Those godly friends in my life reminded me why it is important to stick to my biblical convictions and reminded me of my worth in Christ.

Second Timothy 2:22 tells us to "Flee also youthful lusts: but follow righteousness, faith, charity, peace, with them that call on the Lord out of a pure heart" (KJV). I memorized this verse as a teenager, and it wasn't until I was much older that I forgot the most essential piece of this puzzle. Many of us simply aim to avoid lust. We avoid sin, we avoid temptation, or we avoid things that are harmful. There's nothing wrong with avoiding sin; we all know the Bible instructs us to do so (1 Thessalonians 5:22). But what God desires more is for us to pursue righteousness. To avoid darkness, but to stay in His light. He wants us to do that with other like-minded individuals because that is when we learn about the beauty and blessing of community. Godly community helps you in your pursuit of spiritual maturity. These are the people willing to confront us boldly and lovingly when we aren't living according to God's plan for our lives. So let's discuss three simple reasons why all of us need accountability.

1. ENCOURAGEMENT WHEN YOU FEEL DOWN

A life spent following Jesus is very rewarding and a privilege to experience, but if we're honest, there are times we feel discouraged. In those dry seasons, our Enemy would love for us to become isolated and give up on God. Like Elijah, we have run in fear or distress and questioned if God is even on our side. Despite the miracles Elijah saw, he entered a season that was overwhelming, and he thought he was the only true prophet that existed (1 Kings 19). You may feel a similar frustration. *Why even bother living if I'm the only one holding on to these convictions? Why go to church if everyone else has left? Why maintain my purity when everyone else is having sex before marriage? Why hold my peace when everyone else can yell and curse when offended?* Sound familiar yet?

God had to remind Elijah that He had seven thousand other believers who had never bowed to Baal (v. 18). Many of us get discouraged when we feel we are the only ones striving to please God, and still we see nothing but obstacles before us. God also instructed Elijah to go and anoint the next king of Aram and king of Israel. Then He instructed him to go and anoint Elisha to be his successor (v. 16). Not only did God prove to Elijah that there were more believers in the world, but He also made sure that Elijah became a close teacher to someone who would replace him. He was connected. If Elisha was ever tempted to feel as alone as Elijah had, he would have proof from his mentor's experience that Elijah had made it out of that dry season as well. And if Elijah ever felt alone again, he'd know there were others with the same goals he had.

I'm not sure what season of life you are in, but I know that it shouldn't be a season that separates you from God or His people. You may need encouragement and feel as though you're running on empty. Maybe you're constantly pouring into people, but no one seems to care. Like David, we all will encounter moments when we have to encourage ourselves in the Lord (1 Samuel 30:6). Still, there are times we need others to encourage us to keep trusting in God and to keep pushing forward (23:16). It's not good for man to be alone.

2. STRENGTH IN NUMBERS

There are some battles that we may not overcome until we are fighting alongside our brothers and sisters. It's easy to take an independent approach to life, but the Bible shows us that we all experience great benefits when the church is united. What I love about Acts 2 isn't just the fact that God poured out His Spirit and people began speaking in tongues. I think many of us read that chapter and skip over the fact that the Holy Spirit was poured out when believers were "all with one accord in one place" (v. 1 KJV). Before there can be an outpouring of God's Spirit in our churches or families, we must seek unity. We are stronger when we are connected to the body of Christ.

Seeking accountability can be a terrifying thing because we can't know if someone will strengthen us or harshly criticize us. We have to understand that only fear stops us from confessing our sins and issues to other trustworthy brothers and sisters in the body of Christ. Fear isn't a fruit of the Spirit, and it isn't given to us by our heavenly Father (2 Timothy 1:7). We should reject fear because it is the will of God for us to turn to other believers when we need assistance. If you were to succumb to some form of sin, instead of running away from God, you should be able to run to a trusted brother or sister in the faith who will help restore you to the right path (Galatians 6:1). James 5:16 shows us that we should "confess [our] sins to each other and pray for each other so that [we] may be healed."

I once copied a lengthy message to my Notes app on my iPhone. It detailed everything I was struggling with in reference to lust since starting an unequally yoked relationship. I intended to send it to my then girlfriend to explain where I was, but instead of copying and pasting the note into a text to her, I mistakenly pasted it into the caption of a post I made on Godly Dating 101. Yes, God used an imperfect man to create a page to preach on things I still battled. God can use anyone. I didn't realize what had happened until hours later when I saw dozens, if not hundreds, of messages from people saying they were praying for me, encouraging me that God still had a plan for my future and to not give up. Beyond confused, I began to wonder, *What did I post that let everyone know to bind together in prayer for me?* That's when I checked my last post. My heart sank when I read what I wrote and revealed to the public eye. As embarrassed as

I was, I realized that I truly needed that moment. It's true what James 5:16 says: when we are open with our flaws, we can find healing and support.

I knew I had a problem that I never addressed until it got bad. I always wanted help, but the Enemy convinced me that no one would care enough to pray with me. Everyone would shun me. They'd get the Godly Dating 101 ministry shut down and they'd "cancel" me. I was afraid of cancel culture, but God showed me that cancel culture is not kingdom culture. When we are connected to the body of Christ, we build up one another rather than tear one another down with our words or actions (Galatians 5:14–16). I learned that day that no matter how messy my situation may be, God will always put people near me to help me grow into the person He has destined me to be. If you feel as though no one will understand your past, trust me when I say that God does, and He will always place people in your life to teach you how to walk into the person He created you to be. If you have something you're hiding, please understand that God wants to heal you, but sometimes that healing requires a community.

3. HELP GETTING OUT OF SIN

David was a man of great stature and fame. Because he was king, and possibly felt he was "above" everyone else in Israel, he thought he could do whatever he wanted and simply hide his flaws. Fortunately, God sees beyond the surface level, and God loves us too much to allow us to get too comfortable outside of His will. Because of His love for David, God sent a prophet by the name of Nathan to correct David for his adultery with Bathsheba and ordering her husband, Uriah, to be killed to cover up David's mess. Nathan began to tell a story to David that touched David's heart. Nathan described an injustice done to a poor man—a rich man had taken the poor man's only beloved lamb from

> God loves us too much to allow us to get too comfortable outside of His will.

him and killed it. David got frustrated enough to say the man guilty of that sin was worthy of death. But there was only one problem—that story was about David. Nathan proclaimed, "You are that man" who had so wrongly killed Uriah and stolen his wife (2 Samuel 12:1–10). Isn't it shocking how David hid his sin so well that he was willing to see flaws in others and not spot them in himself? If that sounds familiar, it's because all of us tend to spot the sin in others quicker than we see it in our lives. Without Nathan, David would have had a fractured relationship with God, because he had tried to hide a sin from the people that was still visible to God.

In Psalm 51:10, we hear David saying this in prayer: "Create in me a clean heart, O God. Renew a loyal spirit within me." Many of us have read this beautiful psalm of repentance, but let's remember that it all started due to one man being brave enough to correct the king. This psalm was written in response to Nathan's rebuke. He could have been beheaded for calling out the king and speaking against him, but Nathan knew God wanted better out of David. Many of us need a Nathan in our lives. It is possible to pursue the heart of God yet still have secret sins that we need to address. We need that accountability partner we can lean on for guidance in our relationships and to possibly correct us if we are drifting into sin.

In today's culture, we are told that we should love or listen to only those who agree with us and those who affirm us. But the Bible doesn't portray love as agreement. I'm sure Nathan loved David, but his love for God led him to have those uncomfortable conversations with David. Christians today are called hateful, condemning, and even bigots for disagreeing with the sinful lifestyles of this world. Many believe that to love someone means to be tolerant of their lifestyle. But the Word of God says that even God corrects us because He loves us (Proverbs 3:12; Hebrews 12:6). When you are truly accountable to someone, they can correct you when you're out of alignment with the purpose God has for you. Accountability isn't about supporting someone if what you're approving of is not the will of God.

THE DANGERS OF ISOLATION

It's not always easy to find spiritually mature community, but it has been beneficial in my life and in others'. I once had to lean on my mentor, Steven, for help with an issue I was having. When I told Steven my problems, I was expecting him to tell me how much of a mess I am. Instead, he reassured me of my worth in Christ and helped me get to the root of it. I felt as though he was turning our quick IHOP stop into a therapy session. I can't imagine how things would've gone if I remained isolated and kept my issues to myself. Moments like that have taught me that it is okay to reach out for guidance and not try to figure it out on my own. In turn, I have started allowing myself to be more vulnerable with others, so they can know they have a safe space to talk about their issues and receive prayer and guidance if they desire.

When a couple is isolated, they can easily become the Enemy's prey. We allow our hearts to be vulnerable to attacks that could have been prevented with spiritually mature voices in our corner. I'm not telling anyone that they must go on double dates exclusively until married, but I can attest to the fact that I've made wiser decisions when surrounded by mature believers rather than when my flesh just wants to Netflix and chill. What battles are you facing because you won't admit that you need help? Ecclesiastes 4:9–10 tells us that two are better than one and that if one of those two were to fall, the other person would be there to assist them. What do you think happens when we are alone? That's when we are easier targets and susceptible to staying down. We are fulfilling the law of Christ when we help each other by carrying our neighbor's burdens with them (Galatians 6:2).

First Corinthians 12:18–21 says, "Our bodies have many parts, and God has put each part just where he wants it. How strange a body would be if it had only one part! Yes, there are many parts, but only one body. The eye can never say to the hand, 'I don't need you.' The head can't say to the feet, 'I don't need you.'" All believers are a part of the body of Christ. None of us on our own makes up the whole body, but often we act like we do. I'm not talking about someone who is introverted by nature, but about those who simply don't like working with others or connecting to people whom they deem difficult. The thing about various body parts is they can't exist outside of the body. A hand cannot be removed from our body and then be effective, but it has life and is valuable to the rest of the body as long as it is attached. Disconnecting from the body not only harms us, but it leaves a need in the lives of others. God desires to do great things in the church today, and He wants us to be a part of it. Isolating ourselves may not stop God from doing His will, but it will hinder us from being a part of His perfect plan.

I wouldn't want anyone thinking this is a political book, so I won't say the name of the politician I heard this from: he mentioned that he wouldn't go to lunch or get in a vehicle with a woman who wasn't his wife. Now, you may think, *Good job for him maintaining boundaries* (which we will discuss later), or you may be thinking, *Wow, way to be dramatic!* I believe it was wise for him to understand that because of the role he had and the wife God blessed him with, he shouldn't allow himself to get caught in a vulnerable position. Again, I'm not arguing that double dates are the will of God for our lives, but I will say that when God has a plan for your life, you have to be willing to have some form of accountability and avoid dicey situations where others aren't in the vicinity. You may have pure intentions, but accountability isn't about intentions. It's a standard that pushes us to honor God and be an example to this world that there is strength in community. Accountability helps us remember that the person we're dating isn't our property and that we should treat them as God's child—with the utmost care and respect. Self-accountability will also remind us that even if no one will find out what we've done, God still wants us to walk in holiness and integrity.

The quicker we learn to be connected to godly community, the healthier our relationships will be. It's not that we'll change because we are afraid of someone seeing our shortcomings, but when we live with an eternal perspective, we are more concerned with honoring God rather than our flesh. A godly community helps keep a couple and the individuals in it focused on following Jesus instead of being led by hormones.

4

IT'S A HEART MATTER

I (Tovares) have been in the church for as long as I can remember. My parents were saved when I was around four or five years old, so I have always been around people who love Jesus. Despite being in church for most of my life, I don't think I ever truly knew what *purity* meant. I still remember being a child and questioning everything the teacher or pastor said. If I didn't see it in the Bible, I would boldly say, "That's wrong." Because I was seven, you can imagine that many thought I was precious. Others thought I was annoying. But I was inquisitive because I always wanted to know the truth about important subjects. I believe God wants to raise up a generation of believers who do more than "look saved," people who are hungry for more of Him. People who will do more than claim Christianity, but truly love Jesus and aim to follow Him.

When it came to purity, we barely heard anything about it in church. Nothing substantial at least. I'm not saying this to bash where I grew up, because I am very thankful for where God helped me find His truth. But when it came to the topic of purity, it seems like our leadership avoided this subject. All I was taught is exactly what you may have heard growing up. Yup, you guessed it! "No sex before marriage!" Nothing more. Nothing less. Nothing else.

Little emphasis was placed on *why* we shouldn't have sex before marriage, on the importance of waiting, or even how to wait. So whenever someone brought up the idea of purity, I thought it was all about avoiding sex. Unfortunately, we as human beings tend to do the very thing that we are told not to, just because we feel like it. We saw that in the garden of Eden, just as parents probably see it every day in their kids. If we are honest, many of us completely ignored that simple rule of "no sex before marriage" when we were in love and just having fun.

Safa and I were asked once to do a "purity bonfire" with a church we had the privilege to serve in. We had no idea what to expect, but we enjoyed ourselves. We gathered around a campfire and began to talk to kids about the importance of purity and listened to their hearts as they expressed the things they'd gone through. We heard from children at very tender ages in spiritual bondage to perversion, some who were abused as children, and some who were hoping their parents didn't find out about their boyfriend at age nine. It was refreshing to see that they could be vulnerable with us, but it was frightening to see that a vicious cycle was going to repeat itself: a cycle of young people who were passionate about God but struggling in their attempt to honor Jesus with their actions. Loving God, but not giving up the pornography. Being used by God in various ministries, but still not pure in their hearts. Desiring to go to heaven but struggling to let go of the hell on earth that comes from bondage to sexual sin, or the eternal consequences from this lifestyle (1 Corinthians 6:9).

WHAT DOES IT ACTUALLY MEAN TO STAY PURE?

When something is called *pure*, that means it wasn't mixed with or contaminated by another substance. If I gave you a clean cup with water in it, you could consider that pure water. However, if the cup had just a slight hint of dirt on the inside, it would slowly begin to contaminate the cup with all kinds of particles you wouldn't want to drink. It only takes a little dirt to pollute an entire vessel. Remember, Galatians 5:9 tells us that a little leaven is all that's needed to spread throughout the entire batch of dough.

For Christians, being pure means our hearts can't be contaminated by sin or the things that lead us toward destruction. We have to ensure that we aren't still holding on to the world and our sinful nature but are daily striving to be closer to Jesus. None of us is perfect, but it is hard to progress when we won't let go of what God has saved us from. I can admit that this has been my biggest struggle when it comes to sin in my life. We often say, "I can't stop doing *xyz*," but are we really trying to cut some things off? Jesus told us that some things have to be cut off in order for us to live upright lives (Matthew 5:29–30). To get some sins out of our lives, we must be willing to drastically cut them out. When Jesus said to cut off an arm or pluck out an eye that caused us to sin, of course He didn't mean for us to literally maim ourselves. The spiritual lesson He was showing us is that heaven is much greater than temporary passions. While something may feel good, it isn't worth ignoring our walk with God for it. I know it sounds like I'm preaching, but to be honest, God's liberty does come with expectations. Just because we are saved doesn't mean we shouldn't strive for consecration. To be consecrated simply means to be set apart for God's glory. Not that you will never sin again, but you are striving to live in a way that keeps your heart sensitive to God's will. Titus 2:12 says that an aspect of God's grace is to teach us to deny sinful pleasures and godless living.

I've learned that a life of purity requires the right perspective on God. It is impossible to do the will of God or be obedient to His plan if we don't view Him the way He intends. Because of the holiness of God, there is only one expectation for those born again into His kingdom—holiness (1 Peter 1:16). It's not that we are having sex outside of marriage simply because of lust and how bad we are. We are doing it because we don't understand that God is actually Lord over our bodies (1 Corinthians 6:13). We didn't turn back to that ex solely because we were tired of being single; we did it because we honestly don't think God is more than able to exceed our

> Just because we are saved doesn't mean we shouldn't strive for consecration.

expectations in a future relationship. God's holiness makes Him supremely different from anything our hearts and minds could ever understand. It may seem like a difficult expectation to live up to His standard of holiness, but that is why we are given the Holy Spirit. Our lifestyle changes as we allow Him to develop and mature us into His image. He gives us His Spirit to empower us to turn away from desires that are harmful to our well-being. As we reframe our minds and hearts to live holy lives, God will begin to show us that purity is more than avoiding things; it's more about honoring God.

You cannot change your behavior without addressing the underlying issues at the root of sin. Many of us were willing to stop smoking or drinking when we were saved. They told us that Christians shouldn't do certain things like steal or commit adultery, so we simply aimed to stop doing those things. However, our hearts were never truly freed, because we aimed to change our actions and didn't allow God to work on our hearts. That is why many of us are in church but still in bondage to sin. We have decided to treat the symptoms of sin rather than allow God to remove the root of sin in our hearts. A lack of faith and trust in God is at the root of many things we do. That's why our goal with this book is to always help lead you back to His Word, because He is able to direct us as we follow His will. Psalm 119:9 says it like this: "How can a young person stay pure? By obeying your word."

Perhaps you've asked this infamous question: "How far is too far?" Too often we have been lured by the media and culture in their efforts to get us to redefine what it means to be pure.

One may think purity is a legalistic mindset and an effort to "earn salvation," but that's not it at all. Because we are saved, we have been empowered by the Holy Spirit within us to deny ungodliness (Titus 2:11–14). If we have truly been born again as Jesus taught, He has entered us into a process called *sanctification*. In this process He purifies us and changes us through the Bible and our trust in Him. We must understand that the Holy Spirit is aiming to empower us to do more than speak in tongues; He wants us to live holy.

A life of purity requires a life of separation that allows us to walk in obedience to Christ. We've wrongly equated purity with sexuality, but there's much more to it.

PURITY IS ABOUT YOUR HEART AND MIND

I (Tovares) remember growing up in a church where being a virgin was simply expected for young people—especially in a Jamaican, Christian home. I didn't know if everyone was having sex; I just knew we weren't supposed to. You know, because God said not to and all the leaders would probably get mad if you did. Sadly, at times I was aiming to please God out of fear rather than love. To obey God is wise and should never be taken lightly, but the right mindset about why we are obeying is equally important.

Being a virgin in my age group was weird to my unsaved friends, but I knew they would never grasp the reasoning behind it without a relationship with Jesus. I did everything else under the sun, but because I didn't have sex, I assumed that I was doing a great job pleasing God. My unsaved friends didn't even think I was doing all that I could, so surely I was a top-tier Christian. If anyone was having sex, I felt I could look down on them for not loving God as much as I did.

Truthfully speaking, my virginity didn't impress God because my heart still wasn't pure. Yes, I wasn't having sex, but my heart was full of lustful desires. I didn't get anyone pregnant, so I didn't have to worry about leadership speaking to me. I didn't have to get a sexually transmitted disease (STD) check growing up, so I didn't fear others knowing about my relationships. However, my lust was just as bad as that of the person who was having sex. I must have skipped over the verse where Jesus said I'm just as guilty if I'm desiring it in my heart (Matthew 5:27–28).

I still watched pornography: either the explicit version or the shows with inappropriate scenes that implied sex was happening—you know those movies, where it seems like every fifteen minutes they must imply something sexual. You may be reading this and thinking, *Tovares, you were terrible. No one needed this confession.* I agree to an extent. I was terrible, but His grace was able to restore me. But I disagree that no one needs to hear my testimony! I know there are virgins all around the world who are struggling with lust just like I did. People who are "proud virgins," but their minds have been distorted by the lies of the Enemy. They're possibly walking around in pride because they haven't done anything physically, but their hearts aren't necessarily pleasing God.

And some of you think it's perfectly fine to watch inappropriate shows or movies, as long as you aren't doing what is in those shows yourselves. You may not feel convicted by the music choices that promote sex outside of marriage and stealing someone's girl, but that would directly contradict the words of Jesus. In Matthew 5:27–28, Jesus said, "Ye have heard that it was said by them of old time, thou shalt not commit adultery: But I say unto you, That whosoever looketh on a woman to lust after her hath committed adultery with her already in his heart" (KJV). He brought a new standard that said if our hearts are thinking and desiring something, that's the same as committing the actions. *Woah! So you mean to tell me that I can be a virgin, and God says my mind can allow me to be just as sinful as the prostitute?* Correct. Purity is more than what happens physically. Purity is a matter of the heart and mind.

> Purity is more than what happens physically. Purity is a matter of the heart and mind.

I felt like I achieved something by simply not going the distance myself. Unfortunately, that's exactly what the Enemy desires from us. He doesn't mind us going to a church building or claiming to love God, just as long as our hearts aren't being transformed. If we don't have the proper perspective on purity, we will never truly value it or see the power that comes along with it. The Enemy wants us to compare ourselves to others so we either feel prideful and above others or feel inferior, like the only person in the world who's struggling. Instead, we need to cling to God and rely on Him, because we are only pure through His sacrifice.

Our chastity isn't a way to impress God, but it is a way to

honor Him. What we allow our hearts and bodies to entertain should be chosen out of worship. Not in an attempt to receive God's approval, but because we are thankful for all He's done in our lives. In Romans 12:1, Paul pleaded with the saints in Rome to present their bodies as a living sacrifice. He was showing them that worship is a lifestyle. It's not wasting our time copying the trends and customs of this world; instead, we should live with pure hearts and minds.

Virginity doesn't excite God; obedience does. God desires His children to obey and trust Him. Obedience gives us an opportunity for us to get closer to Him, because sin and rebellion cause a separation from Him. I emphasize this because I have seen people who were virgins ridicule those who weren't. We shouldn't condemn another believer for making a mistake. Putting down someone for their sin doesn't elevate you in the presence of God. A humble heart is what God looks at before He elevates someone.

The Enemy has used popular voices in our culture to lie to us about what purity truly is. Some of these wrong ideas have even stemmed from within the church. Let's discuss a few of those misconceptions now.

MYTH: WE ARE PURE IN THE SIGHT OF GOD JUST BECAUSE WE AREN'T HAVING SEX.

Safa here. What Tovares is trying to say is that you can be a virgin and not be pure. You may never get in bed with someone, but God is aware of the heart's desires even before the action occurs (Proverbs 21:2). Maybe you didn't touch anyone physically, but God saw the inappropriate images that were being sent late at night. Maybe you never went on a date, but God saw the adultery in your heart when speaking to that married individual.

I hope you all don't mind me being real like this. I just believe it's necessary to get honest with ourselves, because we can never be free while pretending that we are perfect. Yes, you may be saved, but God sees the struggle. Yes, you may pay your tithe and even prophesy, but that doesn't excuse the lust. You may even be a pastor, but that doesn't mean God isn't trying to free you from immorality.

I remember when we produced some merchandise for Godly Dating 101 and received some feedback with one of our designs that read, "My Purity Matters to God." It wasn't that most Christians were thinking we were wrong to say it. Some just informed us that they would love to support us by getting that merch, but they weren't virgins. They felt they would be seen as hypocrites because of their pasts. We were quite shocked because we thought people understood purity mattered in many areas, not just the physical. God aims to cleanse our hearts, minds, thoughts, and environments, not just our physical bodies. What was even more alarming was the fact that God forgave so many of these believers, but they still felt as though their past defined them. When God forgives you of your sin, He does not hold it against you. God is not like the people we see daily who might be petty or immature with forgiveness. When God decides to forgive us of our sins, He doesn't keep throwing them back in our faces or reminding us of our failures and inadequacies. Instead, as high as the heavens are above this earth, that's how great His mercy and love are toward those who reverence Him (Psalm 103:11). Your history does not stop God from loving you or desiring to bless you in the future.

Now don't get me wrong: being a virgin and desiring to wait on God to provide a spouse is biblical and a very respectable thing to strive for. First Thessalonians 4:3 informs us that the will of God is for us to avoid fornication. But when God called us to live a life of purity, He was not simply talking about avoiding sexual sin. He was calling us to live a life of separation from sin in general. Purity is more than what happens in your bedroom. Purity is about what is happening in your heart.

> Purity is more than what happens in your bedroom. Purity is about what is happening in your heart.

God desires to do more than clean up our outward behavior. It's not enough for us to have a thriving relationship with Him or someone else. God desires to work on our hearts. So many believe that if they marry a virgin, they won't have any issues to deal with, but there are plenty of virgins carrying a lot of baggage. God desires to make the virgin pure in the same way He works on the person who was in the world all their lives. Our purity is not found in our righteousness, but it is found in the righteousness of God. If left up to our own plans, we would certainly walk straight into sin. It's only the mercy of God that allows us to be justified through the sacrifice Jesus paid at Calvary.

MYTH: MY BODY, MY CHOICE.

As a mother, I've learned that children can be very unreasonable. Toddlers, to be specific. If I gave my son Zion the opportunity, he would easily eat potato chips and fruit snacks for breakfast, lunch, and dinner. He would have ice cream with every meal, and he would drink only juice. There would be no water in sight and not even the faintest chance that he would choose vegetables. If he had to choose a restaurant, I can guarantee he would be getting his chicken nuggets from Chick-fil-A. Extra Polynesian sauce.

In his mind, there's nothing wrong with his food choices. Who cares about green beans when you can have Doritos? He's under the impression that I'm depriving him of the cool snacks when I cook his dinner every day. Of course, he's just a toddler, and it's cute when he does things like this. But it's up to me as his parent and as someone who loves him to protect him from himself. He doesn't know that if I allowed him to eat all those things every day, it would lead to possible constipation. Or worse, diarrhea. He would have cavities and gingivitis to worry about, not to mention malnutrition. And while he's hyper and runs off all his calories within ten minutes, he has no idea the diseases that could be awaiting him in the years to come: diabetes, hypertension, high cholesterol, and worse. It is his body, and he does have rights, but as my child, he can't simply do whatever he desires. I love him with all my heart and want what is best for him, but I understand that he doesn't always know what is best for himself.

One of the Enemy's favorite ways to deceive a believer is

to allow them to think that they can do as they please simply because God is merciful. Not only is that mindset unbiblical, but it's also damaging to our walk with God. If we are born again, our bodies no longer belong to us. First Corinthians 6:19–20 says, "Don't you realize that your body is the temple of the Holy Spirit, who lives in you and was given to you by God? You do not belong to yourself, for God bought you with a high price. So you must honor God with your body." The sacrifice of Jesus actually gives Him the right to guide us and tell us what we shouldn't indulge in. Not only is that fair, but it is safe. God isn't able to sin, which means He isn't able to sin against His children. As the perfect Father, He only desires what is best for us. Some things He restricts not out of punishment but for our protection. Instead of believing God is rejecting our desires, we must learn that He is redirecting them because He wants what is best for us.

MYTH: IF YOU "LOSE YOUR PURITY," YOU ARE NOW DAMAGED GOODS.

Our adversary is very cunning in how he chooses to attack believers. He aims to lure us into sin, but the moment we choose to entertain his lie, he quickly begins to condemn us. He will make sin look beyond attractive but then make you feel dirty the moment you partake in it. Lucky for us, we don't have to continue in it. The sacrifice that Jesus paid for us on Calvary can cleanse us by faith (Galatians 3:26–27). Society may write you off because of your past, but Jesus isn't afraid of your past.

Society often pushes the notion that it's normal for men to

sleep around, but it's devastating if a woman does. Contrary to popular belief, your spouse won't be perfect just because they're a virgin. Our character and our commitment to serving God together are the things that will help us become better spouses. Someone's sexual history doesn't disqualify them from being a great spouse. Rahab, the former prostitute whom many of us in our shallow hearts might have judged if she'd joined our local assemblies, wasn't excluded from the plan of God. Jesus came from her lineage. Not only can God forgive you of the mess that you were once in, He can bless you with a great spouse and bring a blessing in your future.

We as believers have to remove our sexuality from its pedestal. A godly spouse isn't a reward for good Christian behavior. If God sees fit to allow us to be married, it won't be because we "earned" a spouse. Desiring to be a virgin on your wedding day or remaining celibate until married is something all believers should strive for to please God, not to get a spouse.

WHY PURITY IS SO IMPORTANT

I (Tovares) think the reason it is difficult for us to honor God in our relationships is that we easily forget that everything we do should be for the glory of God. We choose sin over His plan because sometimes we choose our glory, our desires, and our aspirations over His plan. We should aim to be pure not so we can appear holy to others but so we can please God despite what others may think of us. First Corinthians 10:31 says, "Whether therefore ye eat, or drink, or whatsoever ye do, do all to the glory of God" (KJV). In all our actions, our ultimate goal is to honor our heavenly Father.

Abstaining from fornication is much more than honoring your future spouse. I'm not sure where this notion has come from, but the point of purity isn't so we can appear spiritual or somehow become more desirable. Today's generation has become focused on the opinions of others over the perspective of God. We have become consumed with trying either to impress people or to do our best to avoid offending anyone, anyone except God, at least. The Bible tells us that because we are bought with a price, we should glorify God with our bodies (1 Corinthians 6:20). If we get married or remain single, our mindset should be the same: *My life exists to bring glory to this great God who loved me enough to die for my sins.*

While being a virgin or remaining celibate don't guarantee you a spouse, avoiding sexual sin guarantees you will be closer to Jesus due to your obedience to His Word. We must keep our hearts and minds pure in order to approach relationships the way God desires. Jesus made a promise to us that those who are pure in heart will see God (Matthew 5:8). Honoring God must be our main priority. Above the relationships. Above all else, we will see God's will come to pass in our lives as we continue to lean on Him. We will have healthier relationships when God is the foundation instead of sex.

Walking in purity helps us more than we may realize in the moment. One important thing I have learned about purity is that it allows us to avoid a lot of unnecessary baggage. Many times, we are wrestling with various issues in our relationships due to things we've entertained in the past. We have unrealistic and unhealthy desires due to years of porn. We have insecurities in our marriages because of an impure past. We have a ton of drama in our lives because we didn't turn away from harmful things.

To keep ourselves pure, we must be willing to be disciplined, which is simply rejecting what we want now for what we want most later. Living a consecrated life allows you to be the spouse God desires you to be, but it also allows yourself to be a vessel God can use for His glory. Second Timothy 2:20–21 says, "Now in a large house there are not only gold and silver vessels, but also those of wood and clay; some for honorable use and some for dishonorable. So if anyone purifies himself from anything dishonorable, he will be a special instrument, set apart, useful to the Master, prepared for every good work" (CSB).

Many people have the impression that they can live however they choose and still be used by God. Unfortunately, that's not biblical. Your obedience doesn't make God love you more or any less, but our separation from this world does determine our proximity to God (2 Corinthians 6:17–18). A pure heart is one that doesn't allow itself to become ensnared by the world's false promises. Aiming to be pure has allowed me to find new ways to love both my spouse and my neighbor, because purity helps us have a heart like Jesus did.

To some, this purity talk may not be a big concern. But why is that? Society has convinced us that believing in God is okay, but it's a turnoff when we decide to surrender our entire lives to Jesus. Religion has become a fad, but God intended for our lives to be transformed. When you're living a consecrated life, you're witnessing to people before you even share the gospel verbally. When your heart is pure, you're showing your partner a representation of how Jesus loves them and would treat them. Sometimes we are afraid to tell the world that our biblical convictions have led us to let go of certain environments and entertainments. But the world is looking for some form of lasting hope and joy. Your obedience to Jesus allows others to see a difference and eventually turn toward Him (Matthew 5:16). The world is tired of convenient and powerless Christianity. People want to see fewer hypocrites and to see us truly live out what we claim to believe.

I'll be honest with you: there have been many times when I wanted to compromise or simply be casual in my walk with God because I was tired of being the person who wasn't getting invited out. Friends have assumed I judge them because I'm not out partying and sleeping around. But the same people who would mock me for my convictions would turn around and ask me for prayer when there was a sickness in their family. When they were experiencing a devastating breakup, they would ask me for prayer or advice. That's why you should continue striving to please God and be pure in heart—because someone's deliverance is attached to your obedience to God. They may never go to your church, but rest assured they will be watching you. Our trust and obedience to Jesus isn't just for us; it's for those around us.

TWO STEPS TOWARD PURITY

So how do we take practical steps toward total purity in our lives? How do we take purity beyond the body and to the heart? Scripture points out two important ways.

1. SPEND TIME IN GOD'S WORD

One of the greatest assets we've been given by God is still one of the most underutilized among Christians. That is the Word of God. Let me tell you why. Remember, Psalm 119:9 says, "How can a young person stay pure? By obeying your word." Our purity is attached to our obedience to God's Word.

The Word of God is considered a spiritual sword (Ephesians 6:17). Jesus defended himself from Satan using the Word of God (Matthew 4). Despite knowing this, many times we still don't use the Word as we should. Let's be honest: we typically get ourselves into trouble when we aren't obeying what God said to do. Only later do consequences make us realize that we should have obeyed in the beginning. We typically fall into things like lust, gossip, envy, drunkenness, or idolatry when we haven't been spending time with God. It's not easy for us to obey God in an area or command that we've never heard of. Studying the Word of God is necessary if we want to stay pure. We must do more than read it casually. We must immerse ourselves to truly know the God we serve.

Reading the Bible is one thing, but studying and obeying it is another. To be honest, it's easy to consider yourself a "Christian" until it is time to actually obey what the Bible says. My goal isn't to question anyone's salvation, but I want us to understand the words Jesus said to His disciples in John 14:15: "If ye love me, keep my commandments" (KJV).

When Jesus redeemed us, He wasn't calling us to perfect church attendance. Neither did He desire to simply make our lives better. He was aiming to conform us into His image. Where sin caused a division between us and God, Jesus came to restore us. Not knowing what His Word says allows us to continue living in sin, fear, anxiety, or brokenness instead of freedom. Not knowing His Word allows us to choose relationships that lead to bedrooms rather than to marriage. Falling in love with the truth of the Word of God gives us a weapon against temptation. The Word of God teaches us how to treat others and shows us how someone will treat us in a godly relationship.

2. AVOID UNGODLY ENTERTAINMENT

Let me preface this section with clarity. I'm not advocating for anyone to put this book down and burn their television, cancel their Netflix, and set up signs outside of their local movie theater that say "Repent." That isn't why God laid this on my heart. God wants us to know that there are some things we have to be "dramatic" about. Be drastic if it means keeping you closer to Jesus. No one likes being that odd Christian who gets labeled *weird* and who no one wants to eat with at lunch, but we have to understand that we are in a fight for our purity. It's difficult for us to keep that pure heart and mind God gave us if we continuously place things in front of ourselves that grieve the Holy Spirit.

I remember checking out a show that most of my Christian friends enjoyed and recommended. I decided to watch it, and I found it very interesting. (I won't specify which show because I'm not judging anyone who may have watched it.) I was glued. I'm embarrassed to admit that I binged the first season in only a matter of days.

Then came season two. I honestly think most modern directors decide to make their shows family friendly in the beginning, but they twist the direction once they have built a large enough fan base. A show that seemed harmless began to use various sexual innuendos and include provocative scenes that I didn't see in the beginning. Then a show that never had cusswords began to add vulgar language. Eventually I knew this wasn't helping me spiritually and was affecting my mind, so I had to cut it off. I had to fight to have a pure mind.

This is when I finally understood what David meant in Psalm 101:3: "I will refuse to look at anything vile and vulgar. I hate all who deal crookedly; I will have nothing to do with them." Of course, King David didn't have a Netflix account or watch any HBO "after dark" programs. But he made a commitment to God that he wasn't going to place anything inappropriate in front of his eyes. Many of us remember his moments of adultery with Bathsheba, but I think we casually miss what led him down that slippery slope. The issue wasn't that the king was on his rooftop and noticed a woman. The problem was when he allowed himself to become fixated on her as she bathed. As he stared, his body began to desire what his eyes were focused on. The problem isn't necessarily noticing that movies are full of perversion, but intentionally going after them. When we see things that grieve the Holy Spirit inside us, we have to choose to turn away from them.

For our spirit to grow, we should starve our flesh and feed our spirit (Galatians 5:16). I have no control over what culture is doing, but I can choose to honor God. I have no power to interrupt the secular world's agenda to push promiscuity and to normalize sin, but I can choose to not entertain it and guard my heart.

I wouldn't consider myself "old" just yet, but I have learned throughout the years that the media has an agenda that will do one of three things: entertain, educate, or convince. When striving to have a pure heart, we cannot allow ourselves to engage in everything simply because it's accessible. Many things are permissible, but not everything edifies us in the long run (1 Corinthians 10:23).

In my journey to remain pure, adding more godly music to my phone has helped me spiritually. One of the biggest issues God had to break in my life was my addiction to secular hip-hop. I'm not saying you're heading to hell if you are listening to it, because I think none of you can argue with me about J. Cole being the best rapper to exist in my generation. My point is, God had to separate me from my love for some artists because of the message they were pushing. I told myself that I would wait until marriage for sex, but all the songs I listened to mentioned how ladies were convenient for my needs but weren't worth marrying. I claimed to love my neighbor, but I listened to songs that objectified them. I couldn't listen to anything about Jesus in the gym. I mean, let's be real. I'm not trying to fall off the treadmill because I'm crying with my hands up listening to Maverick City Music. But I was making excuses for things that were detrimental to my spiritual growth.

Music influences us, whether we like to admit it or not. If we are listening to Christian music, it makes us want to worship Jesus. If you have ever gone to a cookout, you can expect to hear some old-school jams that will make you want to dance. If you want to hit the gym, you may find something upbeat that can get you in your zone. And I don't mean "Shake It Off" by Taylor Swift.

Music sets a tone and allows our hearts and minds to start thinking about specific things. I refuse to write this book and tell someone it isn't God's will for them to listen to anything except for hymns and Christian music. But I will say that whatever you listen to has the capacity to uplift your spirit or to pull you down. Music can push you closer to the presence of God or pull you away. Ask Saul. His rebellion caused an evil spirit to come and torment him. However, when David would play music in Saul's presence, that spirit would leave Saul (1 Samuel 16:23). If you want to be more aware of God's presence in your life and to realign with Him, it is possible that music could assist in that area.

A FRESH START

I (Safa) want to drive something home for you. We don't aim to be pure in body and mind so we can attain salvation or prove how righteous we are. It doesn't guarantee a spouse, and it doesn't mean we are better than anyone else. We strive for purity so we can truly enjoy our salvation. A heart saturated with Christ is surrounded by true love, joy, and peace. A heart tainted by the things of this world will constantly have to battle stress, insecurities, shame, and sin, none of which God desires for us.

Before we go forward in this book, I believe we should stop and say a prayer of repentance. We should pray like David did in Psalm 51:10: "Create in me a clean heart, O God, and renew a right spirit within me" (ESV). You don't have to put the book down and drive to your local church for this. Repentance doesn't require you to cry in front of the pulpit. Repentance simply means to "think differently" or to "turn back toward God." I believe so many of us in this generation desire a godly marriage, but before we can have that, we must have pure hearts. People want to strengthen their walk with Jesus, but unfortunately, they can't because they have sins in their hearts that they need to confess and repent of (Psalm 66:18). Not that God requires perfection for you to be in relationship with Him, because none of us are "good enough" to earn mercy and forgiveness. But we all need to ask God to search the hidden areas of our hearts. You know that area where no one knows you're struggling? That's the part you need to address before we continue in the book. That's the part of you God is trying to heal before you invite someone else into your own dysfunction and insecurities.

So, let's pray this prayer together.

Heavenly Father, thank You for being such a merciful and loving God. Thank You that even when my conduct and my heart don't please You, You still have Your hand on me. You still desire a relationship with me despite my flaws. Open my eyes to the areas of my life that may be hindering me from growing closer to You. If it is something that I must give up, help me to understand that Your ways are higher than mine, and You wouldn't remove anything from my life that You couldn't replace. Help me let go of my idols so I can be who You called me to be. Allow me to seek You for who You are and not for what You can give. In Jesus' name, amen.

5

THE TRUTH ABOUT SEX

Growing up in Miami, I (Tovares) wasn't afforded the opportunity to go to any campfires. However, our Jamaican culture managed to do something slightly similar. Our home was near a lake, so we had to fight off mosquitoes at night. To combat those bugs, my dad would light a small flame over some bushes, and the smoke would repel them. You might have had OFF! bug spray, but we simply had a lighter and some grass. But my dad couldn't just carelessly burn grass for it to do the trick. He had a system in place, and he taught us that we would always have to be careful so that small flame wouldn't cause an issue and spread elsewhere. Something that is beneficial could also become dangerous if mishandled. It needed a safe space.

When it comes to something as serious as sex, it needs a safe space—and that place is marriage. When we think of fire, we know it is beneficial. But when a fire breaks out in the forest, we know destruction is sure to come. When we think about water, we know it is beneficial. But if a dam breaks or a river surpasses its bounds, floods could cause devastation. Just because something is "good" doesn't mean it can be done outside of God's terms. Sex is pleasurable, but it cannot become our guide. When done God's way, this will help us avoid sinning against Him and our own bodies. Marriage is the safe zone for sex to be rewarding, pleasurable, and holy—free from insecurities and fears. We don't have to waste energy worrying about whether the dating relationship will work; we know the marriage will last because we are doing things God's way.

I remember growing up and not knowing much about how to navigate a sex-driven world. I wanted to honor God, but sin was both permissible and celebrated. Almost every TV show is hypersexualized, presenting things to us that make perversion seem normal. Most of what I learned about sex came from my surrounding culture. I always heard the guys say that they were just trying to get a girl for the night. Marriage wasn't really celebrated in my neighborhood. There were more single-parent homes or divorced parents than I could count. I would see many young women pregnant, but no father in sight. Unfortunately, many of them bought the lie that sex was an activity and not something holy that we should value. God always intended us to view sex as a gift for married couples, but society has trained us to think that it is something we simply do with whoever we are dating or whoever we meet on an app. So many of us think sex is something we do because we are "grown," and for the person who complimented us without commitment, but we ignore the fact that God designed it for the marriage bed.

TEACHING ABOUT SEX SHOULDN'T BE TABOO

The body of Christ hasn't always done a great job in approaching this topic with the younger generation. I believe a major problem the church has wrestled with is how to properly address sex in a healthy and realistic manner. We can't yell, "No sex!" in someone's ear for years, then see them after their honeymoon and assume they felt okay embracing the sexuality God gave them. We must adopt a more godly approach to this. Sex outside of marriage is ravaging our churches, especially our young adults. Many marriages in the church have failed due to infidelity. Many young people have turned away from Jesus because of sex outside of marriage. Let's keep it real for a moment: many dating relationships should have ended ages ago, but people stay and hope for the best simply because the sex is great. Sex is impacting our world more than we may want to admit.

I have realized over the years that to learn a subject properly, we need to have the right teachers. When we allow our unsaved friends at school or work to be our guides for sex, we end up in bed with people we never committed to or simply having sex because "everyone else is doing it." God forbid we learn from modern artists and actors. It appears that Hollywood has a vile plan to eliminate anything pure about sex and simply encourage people to do whatever and whoever they want. It's obvious that the world is very opinionated, but cultural opinions have become the "truth" for today's generation. Most of what our youth learn isn't coming from the Bible or solid, biblical leadership. We must become proactive as believers in changing that narrative, because who we allow to teach our children will either point them toward Christ or toward another relationship that leaves them feeling empty. It's time for the church to speak up and shed light on what the Word of God says.

Who was your first teacher in regard to sex? I pray that you could say your parents or pastor. However, many of us learned all that we know through avenues that weren't Spirit led. My first time hearing anything about sex was when I was watching HBO "after dark." I was growing up in a home with godly parents but sneaking to watch inappropriate things with my brothers late in the night. Maybe you've been there also: watching *BET: Uncut* but keeping the previous channel on ESPN or TBN. If someone walked in, no big deal. I just pushed the "previous" button, and no one would realize I was trying to learn about sex from an outlet that had a much different view than Scripture on what sex means. Looking back, I'm surprised that my urges and hormones didn't drive me to cause more damage to myself than they did.

There has been a constant rise in perversion in our culture that has skewed the minds of the masses in regard to sex. The world says, "It's just sex," but the Bible shows us sex is for marriage. Culture tells us we're not in a real relationship until sex is involved, but God's Word shows us that we need to keep Him involved. As the body of Christ, we must learn what God says on the subject and be willing to talk about it as loudly as we do with other subjects. Because God's way is more fulfilling and leads to true joy.

THAT'S NOT TRUE

There are so many different teachings we've heard about sex that didn't originate from God's Word. I (Safa) believe it's time to debunk some of these myths and establish some solid ground for you to stand on. Let's start with talking about a few myths we've all been taught about sex, whether they're from church or from our culture.

MYTH: WE SHOULD AVOID SEX.

Growing up, I heard leaders with good intentions tell me that I should avoid sex. I get their point, but that's just not biblical. We shouldn't necessarily avoid sex; we should avoid fornication. Sex isn't the problem; immorality is. If we tell people to avoid sex, that means we are telling people to avoid marriage. Sex, when performed in God's holy covenant called marriage, is a blessing. Sex is a gift, and I believe the words we use when talking about it show the value we place on what God instituted. The problem arises when we try to get God's blessing outside of His context—marriage. Countless people today aren't having sex outside of marriage but are still entertaining fornication. They may be virgins, but they still battle with lust. Now before you call me crazy, let me explain.

When Paul instructed us to "flee fornication" in 1 Corinthians 6:18 (KJV), he wasn't speaking solely about sex with the person that you're dating. With our twenty-first century mindset, we have simply assumed he was only saying to physically not have sex with someone you're not married to. In Greek, the word we translate as *fornication* is *porneia*. This is also where we get our English word *porn* or *pornography*. Paul was ultimately telling the believers in Corinth to avoid any thing that was promiscuous in any way. We can take that as direct advice to the church today. If there is a film that would be considered inappropriate, Paul would urge them to avoid it. If the relationship they were entertaining could lead to sex prior to marriage, he'd say to run away from that. If the conversations they were having were pushing them toward sexual temptation, Paul would want them to turn into Usain Bolt and run as fast as they could away from it. And ladies, we all know there are some books that have those same effects on us. Often, people preach against sex outside of marriage, but the perspective God wants us to have is much different. Paul actually told the church in Ephesus that they shouldn't even have a hint of immorality or impurity named among them as the children of God (Ephesians 5:3). Many of us have ignorantly presented sex as the problem rather than confronting the real issue—lust and perversion. Lust will cause us to objectify others rather than viewing them as children of God. God's standard is to avoid all forms of lust, not just "avoid sex." When God calls us to a lifestyle of holiness, He wants us to turn away from sin, not label what He created as unclean.

Sex isn't dirty. Sex is beautiful when it is done in the way that God designed—through the covenant of marriage. Personally, for me, sex after marriage was great, but it didn't feel "holy" or seem to me that God was pleased. We both struggled for a while trying to view sex as something that was okay to do because of how we heard it presented in the church growing up. It felt like we had to restrict ourselves from embracing the moment because I had always heard how we needed to avoid sex and that it's a sin. Tovares clearly got over it faster than I did. Guys are weird. But when the church pushes sex as something that is bad, it is difficult for many married couples to simply "flip the switch." Embracing your sexuality is difficult if you don't think your sex drive is from God. Enjoying sex can become burdensome if you forget that God is the One who created it. It becomes pleasurable, holy even, when you understand that it is a form of intimacy that God approves of.

Genesis 2:25 says about Adam and Eve, "They were both naked, the man and his wife, and were not ashamed" (KJV). It's the will of God for you to be vulnerable with your spouse and not feel the need to walk in shame. Theologically speaking, this is the form of living that God wants us to return to. Many youth were told to simply avoid sex, but when they stumbled into perversion, many of them never came out of it. Why? It didn't seem as bad as they expected. They enjoyed the moment, and that caused them to resent the church rather than understand what was happening. If they had been taught that sex is beautiful and taught why we should wait, they would be more inclined to trust God's timing instead of experimenting when the leaders weren't looking. For years, people were shamed for having a child out of wedlock. While fornication is a sin, simply condemning those who were caught didn't solve our sin problem. It simply led to Christians being more secretive in their actions. The sin never stopped; there were just more church members purchasing Plan B pills and even getting abortions. I believe all that was rooted in the fact that we never truly understood the purpose and beauty of sex. We just understood the rules and how to "look saved." We have to understand that the Bible points us toward reality. Sex outside of marriage clouds our judgment toward that person and creates emotional attachments—not to mention the unwanted pregnancies, broken relationships, and the host of health issues it can present.

It isn't the will of God for you to simply avoid sex, because God has a beautiful purpose for it: reproduction, pleasure, and unification in a marriage. What we must run away from is any form of sexual temptation that tries to interrupt God's sanctification process in our lives (1 Thessalonians 4:3–8). Sex is incredible and meant to be valued. Fornication and lust are the problem.

MYTH: WE CAN HAVE SEX WITH NO STRINGS ATTACHED.

When God gave us the gift of sex, He intended it to both unite and reproduce. Unfortunately, the only benefit society seems to value is the pleasure aspect. They don't mind the orgasm and the climax, but they aren't willing to embrace the wedding ring and covenant of marriage first. We get the impression that it's possible to lie in bed with someone as a form of transaction, and that should be enough. We're told that we can have sex without emotions and it doesn't leave a lasting imprint on both individuals involved. That couldn't be further from the truth. There are always strings attached. Soul-ties may not be a concept many people believe in, but God created our minds and bodies, our hormones, and our hearts to respond to sex as a way to form a bond, not simply experience fun.

The thought process that we can pursue sex solely for pleasure while separating it from God's original intent causes countless problems in our world. Studies prove that the United States has the world's highest rate of children living in single-parent homes. Almost a quarter (23 percent) of our youth under the age of eighteen only live with one parent.[1] Even though not everyone who has sex outside of marriage ends up with children, they still place themselves at risk for STDs, broken hearts, and wasted time. Sex was not created to be solely recreational; it is how God decided to bond together two individuals. So, while many are thinking there will be no connections after they get out of the bed, a merging still took place. They might not have gone to the altar to become a legally married couple, but according to Genesis 2:24, God unites us as one flesh during sex. Even if we don't notice it, we spiritually intertwined our souls to someone whom God probably didn't want us to associate with. The relationship may not last, but those strings will remain.

FRIENDS WITH BENEFITS

There was a time when I (Tovares) was so casual in my walk with God that I truly didn't care to obey His Word. Not that I am perfect now, but there was a point when I undoubtedly started to ignore God and do my own thing. I remember being with a young lady just because I wanted to. She looked nice and she was interested, so I went for it. The guilt and shame really kicked in after we had sex, and I couldn't live with myself. Afterward, she continued to reach out. I explained to her why I couldn't start that type of relationship. That wasn't what I desired in my future. I expected her to either mock my beliefs or say that we should start dating, but her response took me aback. She told me that no relationship would be needed but asked if we could continue to have sex. Astonished by her answer, I just continued to make up excuses and avoid her until she stopped asking.

She wasn't offended that we had sex and I didn't love her. Neither did she seem to care that I wasn't aiming to pursue marriage with her. We had no connection emotionally or spiritually, and it didn't bother her. The part that shocked me was that she was fine with us continuing to be physically intimate, knowing I didn't love her. That's when I realized that I had started the relationship solely to selfishly meet my desires rather than pursue commitment. I didn't think about how she would feel before initiating that connection. I was focused on how she, or any woman for that matter, could help me feel satisfied momentarily, but deep down I didn't desire to love her the way she deserved as God's creation. It's appalling to see how many of us have taken something as sacred as sex and turned it into something we simply do for fun. Something that we do because it's pleasurable, but not holding it in high value the way God does. Not desiring to be fully known and fully loved, but simply to enjoy moments of fun. That made me even more devastated to see how I allowed myself to fall into the Enemy's game. Sex is a blessing, and it isn't something that we should be careless with. My actions didn't honor God and never truly honored that young woman, who ended up being used and mistreated.

Boyfriends shouldn't get husband privileges, and girlfriends shouldn't expect to get husband blessings until after the wedding day. Proverbs 5:15–17 says it like this:

> Drink water from your own well—share your love only with your wife. Why spill the water of your springs in the streets, having sex with just anyone? You should reserve it for yourselves. Never share it with strangers.

To be honest, if you are being coerced into sex with someone, they shouldn't be considered your friend anyway. A friend is supposed to value you, love you, correct you when you're wrong, build you up, and be there for you when you need it. Friends who are simply looking for benefits do not value your friendship; they value what they can get from you.

Some have allowed these unhealthy friendships into their lives due to a desire for companionship, but true intimacy requires commitment. Maybe you desired a relationship, but you went along with the friends-with-benefits (FWB) dynamic because you wanted to keep someone close. Desiring some fun? You can call them up. Bored and in need of something to do? They're one text away. But those moments of fun won't lead to commitment or love. They lead to us giving pieces of ourselves away to people who don't love us enough to wait until marriage. They lead us to becoming one with multiple people, because the Bible shows us that sex is like a form of glue (1 Corinthians 6:16). You two may stop being FWB over a disagreement or because you've simply matured, but as Safa explained, those "benefits" made you connected to them in the sight of God.

Your heart is of too much value to God for you to settle as a backup plan. You're too precious in the sight of our heavenly Father for you to settle as their plan B when the person they really desired ignores them. You don't want to have strings attached to people who won't decide to be in covenant with you. It's never worth it.

"No strings attached" always seems promising in the beginning, but it never delivers for various reasons. One reason is that God created us for relationship. To think that we can constantly have sex without developing feelings for the other person is absurd. It places our hearts on the line to be broken, because we will desire commitment and not receive it. You end up jealous, bitter, or envious when they find someone they want to marry and that person isn't you. After all those moments in bed, it's not enough for a ring.

MYTH: SEX BY ITSELF CAN SUSTAIN RELATIONSHIPS.

I (Tovares) remember being in the military and associating with people I knew I shouldn't have been close friends with. I had a friend who started seeing another woman in the military, and he asked a group of us what we thought about her. None of us approved, because we knew it was only sex that kept them together. They had nothing in common it seemed, but they just decided to stay together for the sex.

Unfortunately, she wasn't faithful to him, and then she dumped him when he found out about it. He was devastated. He genuinely thought the amount of sex they were having meant the relationship was healthy. How could she not truly love or respect him if they were always in bed together? But the problem with that mindset is that sex isn't a strong enough foundation to build a meaningful relationship on. Only Jesus is. What many of us fail to realize is that sex outside of God's proper context, marriage, actually clouds our judgment. While we are thinking that this person surely must be the will of God for our lives, they are just a distraction. While we are on cloud nine and excited to be in a new relationship, it's really the orgasm that has blinded us to the fact that they have been pulling us away from our biblical convictions.

Our generation has tried to create a hookup culture that tells us it is okay to simply connect to just anyone, but that isn't what God desires for any of us. He designed sex to unite a man and a woman together in marriage. When we take the beauty of that and pass it around to whoever makes us happy, we find that our relationships are shallow and empty, not edifying us or bringing out the best in us. It's selfish, to be honest. When God proved His love for us, He didn't do so by taking things away; He did it by giving. He gave Himself as the ultimate sacrifice so we could find love, joy, peace, and eternal life (John 3:16). Any relationship based on what you can gain from the other person instead of serving them isn't a relationship God approves of.

Let's pick back up on the Bible story of Amnon and Tamar that we touched on earlier. King David had a beautiful daughter by the name of Tamar, and she had a half-brother by the name of Amnon. He became obsessed with her to the point that it made him sick. Day after day he would see her beauty and become frustrated that he couldn't have her. Unfortunately, he had a friend named Jonadab (remember him?) who was a horrible influence in his life. Jonadab saw how frustrated Amnon appeared to be, so he inquired about what was causing his discouragement. Amnon explained that he was in love with his sister and knew he shouldn't have her. Jonadab got him to pretend to be sick, so he could take advantage of her when she was trying to help him feel better. When Tamar was so kindly looking after her brother, he forced himself on her despite her efforts to stop him. She begged Amnon not to kick her out and further disrespect her. However, the Bible says that Amnon's love for Tamar turned into hatred (2 Samuel 13:15). His hatred for her was even stronger than the "love" he claimed to have in the beginning.

We know that any incestuous relationship is wrong, but this story highlights an important truth: sex was not created to be the foundation for a relationship. When a relationship is built on lust and perversion, it isn't strong enough to last. Amnon's love for Tamar became nonexistent after he got what he desired all along. It's like a man or woman who flatters you for weeks, but they dump you after sex. Or the one-night stand that you wanted to lead into more, but they asked you to leave their home after their Netflix-and-chill moment reached its end.

God didn't design sex to be casual. Sex should be the icing on the cake within marriage, instead of the cake itself. If there is no bond outside of sex, the relationship will fail.

A FEW TRUTHS ABOUT SEX

We all need a renewed mind toward sex so we can start seeing the beauty God created in it rather than the way our culture has distorted and weaponized it. So we turn from the sinking sand of the myths above to stand firmly on the following truths.

TRUTH: SEX IS GOD'S IDEA.

I (Tovares) would assume that the very first thing God was concerned about teaching humanity was the importance of worship or something about holiness. But Genesis 1:28 says, "And God blessed them, and God said unto them, Be fruitful, and multiply, and replenish the earth, and subdue it: and have dominion over the fish of the sea, and over the fowl of the air, and over every living thing that moveth upon the earth" (KJV). God decided to create mankind and immediately tell them to reproduce. Sex isn't something the Enemy formulated to give to us, but God was the One who, in His wisdom, decided to allow us to enjoy that experience. Sex was never our issue, but what we learned about it has taken us in a wrong direction. Since God is the Creator of sex, it is good, like everything else He created. Our world, and the church, too, may have an ungodly view of sex, but it is a beautiful thing in His eyes. God has always had a good intention for sex: to join a man and wife together physically, emotionally, and spiritually.

When God designed sex, He planned for it to be the way that we reproduce here on earth and connect to our spouse. He could've made it a mundane process that left no fulfillment, but He decided to have us enjoy it as well.

TRUTH: SEX WILL CONNECT US EMOTIONALLY.

Genesis 2:25 informs us that when Adam and Eve were together and naked, they felt no shame. Vulnerability allows us to be fully known through sex. When God created Adam and Eve, there was nothing they had to worry about hiding from the other. The purity of sex allows us to unite without having to be defensive or feel unsafe. Being naked in marriage is more than being undressed physically—it's being open and transparent in all areas of our lives.

A hormone called oxytocin is often released during sex. With this hormone, a bonding takes place that connects you to the other individual. It doesn't matter if you thought they were the worst-looking person in history; if the relationship is consensual, this hormone can make you think they're the best thing since sliced bread. This hormone is also passed from mother to child through lactation.[2] It is why many claim they are only participating in a one-night stand, but they'll actually be emotionally connected to that individual long after the sex is over. When done in marriage, sex will strengthen our union in more ways than we realize.

TRUTH: SEX CAUSES A SPIRITUAL COVENANT.

In 1 Corinthians 6:15–16, Paul taught us an important concept about sex. He informed us that if we were to lie in bed with a prostitute, that sexual moment would actually make us one with them. Verse 16 says it like this: "The two are united into one." That shows us that we have a responsibility to uphold. If we don't want to form a spiritual covenant with someone, we shouldn't have sex with them.

When God created sex, He wanted us to truly experience unity in its deepest form. God said the "two shall become one" when He spoke of sex (Mark 10:8 ESV). In the Bible, a marriage became validated once it was consummated through sex. Today, we think we have to date, get engaged, sign paperwork at the courthouse, get a big wedding at church, then honeymoon in Cozumel, Mexico, before God sees an actual union. Actually, God recognizes a spiritual covenant once there is sex. I know the idea of the soul-tie isn't necessarily a biblical concept, but we must process that when God created sex, He intended it to tie your soul together with your spouse's. We must be careful not to "become one" with someone we aren't married to. You may break up, but God still recognizes the "marriage" you created.

When Paul spoke of being "united" to our spouse in Ephesians 5:31–32, he meant more than living together. God's plan for marriage was for the married couple to adhere to one another like glue. The holy act of sex would consummate their union and bond them in a way that should only be separated by death. Our earthly minds will never truly grasp all God's mysteries, but God gives us a slight glimpse of His true love in a way that we can understand through earthly things like marriage. There is no point at which we are closer to an individual than when having sex. To think that we can separate sex from covenant is not only unwise but impossible. Sex will connect us on a deeper level, and when we take a casual approach to it, we miss out on the blessings that God desires us to have. This is why we see the Enemy attacking so many marriages. He aims to push you toward sex when single, but he aims to drive you apart after marriage. Our adversary understands that there is power in a spiritual covenant that God approves of, so he tries to get us to mishandle this blessing.

THE IDOLATRY OF SEX

There is only one thing we should pursue every single day, and that is God Himself. Outside of Him, no person or thing should be our ultimate priority and desire in life. Despite our understanding that sex is a blessing, our society has perverted that blessing and turned it into an idol. This reminds me of the bronze serpent Moses created in the Bible. It was a blessing and something that started out pure. Throughout the book of Numbers, the children of Israel were constantly nagging and complaining against Moses and God. Due to their negativity, God allowed them to be attacked by venomous snakes. When they repented,

God told Moses to build this bronze serpent, and whenever the people were poisoned from a bite, they would find healing by simply looking to this serpent. Jesus Himself alluded to His death on the cross by referring to the bronze serpent (John 3:14–15). Unfortunately, over time the Israelites began to worship it as though it were God. King Hezekiah had to destroy the serpent to stop them from worshipping that idol. The Bible warns us to keep away from idols (1 John 5:21). God warns us against idolatry not just because He's a God with a jealous heart, but because no one, nothing, can fulfill us the way He can, and He desires what is best for us. God's jealousy is righteous, because He understands that anything we worship outside of Him will lead to our destruction.

Sex has become easier to get, but love is still hard to find. Sex has become more accessible, but people still aren't experiencing true intimacy. It's on our phones, it's in every song, and it's displayed in every ad. Society has become sex crazed, to say the least. Children can't watch cartoons without being interrupted by a new character "coming out of the closet." We can't watch an NFL or NBA game without a half-naked actress promoting something as simple as a cheeseburger on the commercial break. Does sex sell? Sadly it does, but sex outside of marriage does more than sell financially; it aims to rob us of our identity. Sex outside of God's context will cause us to compromise who God created us to be in exchange for moments of pleasure. Sex in marriage is symbolic of us being united with one person without having to deal with shame or compromising in our walk with Jesus.

But let's address the real elephant in the room that's attacking the church as a whole. Often it has been presented as a male issue, but women struggle as well. Even leaders in the church. Children we are afraid to teach about this mature subject are being exposed to it: porn.

PORNOGRAPHY

I (Tovares) was exposed to pornography as a child, so I came to think sexual entertainment wasn't that bad. But Hebrews 13:4 says, "Marriage is honourable in all, and the bed undefiled: but whoremongers and adulterers God will judge" (KJV). I realize now that sex wasn't meant to be someone else's entertainment but a way to unite a man and a woman in marriage. It's supposed to be "honorable" and "undefiled," not a commodity. We are bombarded with the cheapened version of sex in almost every ad, social post, TV show, movie, song, and, of course, pornography.[3] This industry wants viewers to believe they're just supplying a need, but porn is actually a health crisis that is harming us more than we've realized. Porn is leading us to believe what we are seeing is real or a form of love—neither of which is true. Many are in bondage to masturbation, depression, anxiety, and mental health issues due to the way this form of media has given them an ungodly view of sex. When we allow pornography to be our teacher, sex becomes something that's violent, that focuses on being served rather than serving, and that leads to a flawed view of God's reality. Porn turns sex into a transaction, and people become objects.

It's possible that someone reading this will believe that I am only against pornography because I am a Christian. But studies have shown that there are scientific reasons we would all benefit from avoiding porn. "Just like addictive products such as tobacco, porn can create pathways within the brain that lead to cravings, and those cravings can push consumers to search longer and more diligently for the same level of 'high.'"[4] Porn is addictive and destructive. "Just this once" sounds great, but it is not realistic. Thankfully, God can break the chains of any addiction we may have.

To break free from these issues, we must do more than "not have sex." No one is going to break free from their idolization of sex or from the gruesome hold of pornography by simply attending more church services. We need the power of the Holy Spirit to destroy the chains in our hearts and minds (Isaiah 10:27). We need to embrace the *proper* view of God. We must learn to see God through the right perspective, so we see that He isn't aiming to restrict us from "fun," but trying to prevent us from harming ourselves. We didn't pursue sex solely because we have an issue with lust; we forgot that Christ is Lord over our bodies.

In 1 Corinthians 6:19–20, Paul taught us that we are the temple of the Holy Spirit and that we were bought with a high price, so that means we must honor God with our bodies. Our bodies should glorify God—not so we can earn His salvation, but because we are His. If we profess to be believers, we must understand that we are actually saying our bodies no longer belong to us. We are saying that even if we desire sex, we won't rush to do it outside of God's context. We want everything we do to bring glory to God in some way (Colossians 3:17). Often, the only thing receiving glory when we have sex is our flesh. That's what our Enemy desires. He only wants us to pursue something that is holy as long as it's outside of God's parameters. Instead of following our urges or the ideologies of our culture, we must follow Christ and His plan for our lives.

FOLLOW THE MANUAL

I hate buying things that require me to follow instructions. I'm mature enough to admit my weaknesses, and I am convinced that I'm the furthest thing from a handyman. I didn't even like watching *Bob the Builder* that much growing up. I will gladly spend money for someone else to build something if the instructions aren't self-explanatory. That seems to be what most males are like when we have manuals with too many guidelines to follow. We just like getting straight to the point. Safa, on the other hand, is willing to build anything. I'm convinced that if she wanted to build a house, she could. Just give her a manual, the material, and a little bit of time. She will figure it out. She knows I always call her "Bobbesha the Builder." Nickelodeon or HGTV can feel free to sponsor her whenever they are ready.

My stubbornness when it comes to following manuals usually causes situations to end unfavorably. Safa loves shopping at IKEA, and I have to agree that they have some really great products. But IKEA is a store where almost all the products require assembly. Needless to say, I wasn't fond of our purchases. I built a dresser for us to share, and to this day one of the drawers doesn't work as it should—not because the product was defective, but because I wanted to build it without following instructions. We are both aware that we have to replace our kitchen chairs because those chairs I assembled shouldn't feel like rocking chairs. Those unused screws were for decoration, right?

While it may be okay to simply wing it when you're building a chair, that isn't the mindset we should have within our relationships. When it comes to sex, I think many of us take that same careless approach. When we have sex with whomever we love at the moment, we simply do what we believe works best for us. I mean, that would be okay if we actually knew what was best for us. Unfortunately, our emotions and urges aren't safe enough to be our guide. "Follow your heart" is society's ethos, but the Bible tells us that isn't wise. Again, Jeremiah 17:9 says it like this: "The heart is deceitful above all things, and desperately wicked: who can know it?" (KJV). Our culture may tell us to trust our hearts, but, again, the heart isn't the most reliable source to trust. The best place to look when we are wondering how to navigate sex is to understand what the Creator of it says. We need to understand what the "manual," the Word of God, says so we won't harm ourselves or others. Just like a fire can do more harm than good, sex outside of God's design of marriage will do more harm than good. But when done correctly, it is both pleasurable to the Creator and to the married couple.

BOUNDARIES ARE BLESSINGS

For five and a half years of my life, I (Tovares) had the privilege to serve in the United States Navy. I gained some experiences I will remember for a lifetime. Some of those were great, and some I was glad to be done with. Many might think that the most frustrating thing I had to go through was my deployment. As exhausting as that time was, that deployment only lasted half a year. And the physical fitness aspect was not what I complained about the most. Having to wake up at 5:00 in the morning to get to physical training by 5:30 was tiring, but I knew we had to be physically fit for the mission ahead.

The part of my military career I think was the most annoying and tedious was having to go through security at the gate every single day. That's right. This was more annoying than boot camp on some days. Whenever I wanted to get on base, I had to get checked to ensure I was actually qualified to be there. I could be in full uniform, drive for thirty minutes to get to my base, wait in line behind dozens of vehicles, and then not get access if I didn't have my common access card (CAC). That ID card was your key to access the base. Without it, it did not matter if you were late or early; you weren't getting on. I could be going to the base for work, the gym, the grocery store, or because I had something to do that would take only five minutes; it didn't matter. I was going to get my credentials checked. If I didn't have my military ID with me, it meant I was not going to get past the gate.

To the military members running late for work due to over-sleeping or stopping at Starbucks, that gate can be a disturbing experience. You just want to get to your shift on time, but the gate was very often backed up with only one person checking IDs.

While I didn't value them at the time, those security guards were some of the most essential workers on our base. Without them, anyone with the desire to go on the base could've easily strolled in. Random civilians who may have even meant us harm could have jumped right in and done some unspeakable things if they weren't investigated by security. I believe that it is imperative to safeguard anything that we value. My brother was actually a part of that navy security team (master-at-arms) at the gate. I vividly recall some days when he didn't care to be there himself, but people like him and his coworkers have surely prevented many base attacks.

The older I get, the more I am convinced that this is how life works for us believers spiritually and emotionally as well. When there is no "gate" to protect our hearts, bodies, or spiritual lives, we allow ourselves to give access to people who have no business being in our lives. Proverbs 23:10 tells us, "Don't cheat your neighbor by moving the ancient boundary markers." What does that mean? Moving the boundaries would be stealing the land. A lack of boundaries is like an invitation to steal what we value. When we lack boundaries, we allow other people or our weaknesses to create a standard for us in difficult moments. We unknowingly allow people to determine the course of our lives. The military knew we needed security before a crime occurred, not after. Likewise, we must create boundaries before sin is birthed. If we wait to create boundaries until we are tempted, we've allowed our lives to be led by the flesh rather than the Holy Spirit.

WHAT ARE HEALTHY BOUNDARIES?

A boundary is a line that draws a limit on an area. Boundaries are implemented because we want to protect either what we have inside from getting out or from something else coming in. We all have those lines that divide our home from the house next door. Without them, your neighbor could stroll over at any point. Healthy boundaries are necessary in the life of every believer.

I (Tovares) remember seeing a boundary sign on a home near my church once. It read, "Trespassers will be shot. Survivors will be shot again." As hilarious and hostile as it was, I understood the owners' sentiment. They wanted to be left alone, and they wanted others to know that there would be consequences if they felt their privacy was being violated. You may not have that sign in front of your home, but if you're a parent, you can understand why they were so adamant about protecting their property. Whether it was their children or possessions, the owners had something they weren't planning to share with strangers or those who might mean them harm.

Do you have any signs up above your heart? Not that I'm saying you need to announce to anyone they will be shot for playing with your emotions, but I need to ask: Is your heart as guarded as it should be? As someone with the Holy Spirit dwelling within you, are you taking the precautionary steps to guard your heart and mind from being infiltrated by people who aren't a part of your story? Don't allow what God deposited into your heart to seep out or be taken away. We often use boundaries for the things we value: security systems are in our homes, and some people choose to live in gated communities. Password biosecurity checks are required for our laptops and mobile devices. I know it's important to keep our personal belongings and information private, but do we guard our hearts the same way? We can't afford to be casual with them.

THE FIRST BOUNDARY EVER

To understand the importance of boundaries, we must first understand who God is. The Bible shows us that one of the greatest ways to describe our God is that He is *holy* (Revelation 4:8). To be holy is to be pure and set apart. His purity and holiness set

Him apart from this world He has created. As we've discussed before, God desires for us to walk in purity also.

Again, we apply boundaries to protect us and those around us. As followers of Christ, we have the greatest treasure we could ever gain. The Spirit of God dwelling within us is something that the greatest riches couldn't purchase and our behavior couldn't earn. Nothing we ever possess will be of more value than the Holy Spirit living within our hearts. Because God allows His Spirit to dwell within us, we have to guard our hearts instead of letting others dictate our lives.

Genesis 2:15–17 describes the world's first boundary: "The LORD God placed the man in the Garden of Eden to tend and watch over it. But the LORD God warned him, 'You may freely eat the fruit of every tree in the garden—except the tree of the knowledge of good and evil. If you eat its fruit, you are sure to die.'" In this exchange between God and Adam, we can see three things happening: God placed Adam in the garden He created, God established privileges and boundaries, and God set consequences if those boundaries were crossed. I'm not sure how many days, weeks, or years went by before Adam and Eve fell into sin, but I do know that God wasn't joking when He said that disobedience would have consequences.

One thing I've noticed about the devil is that he will find the one thing God tells us to avoid and try to convince us to partake in it. We have so much liberty in Christ, but he will try to get us to think that when God says to avoid something, it's because God doesn't love us or want what is best for us. Adam and Eve had free access to everything God created, but they chose to go after the one thing He said to avoid. Sometimes it is a very easy process for us to ignore our boundaries and find ourselves doing things we didn't care to do before we started listening to the wrong voices. Our world wouldn't have experienced death if Adam and Eve had abided by the boundaries God implemented for them. Their fall shows me that the lives of others are depending on our faithfulness to God and the boundaries He desires for us to keep.

HOW FAR IS TOO FAR?

I (Safa) have heard a common question from young adults about setting boundaries. They always ask me essentially, "How far is too far?"

"Is kissing a sin?"

"What can we do and it not be a sin?"

"Can I spend the night with my significant other if I can guarantee nothing will happen?"

Quite frankly, if we begin asking ourselves these questions, we've already missed the point. We aren't setting boundaries so we can toe the line in our walk with Jesus, but we are creating these guardrails so we can remain close to Him. When I think of someone who had healthy boundaries in the Bible, I think of Joseph. Joseph was placed in a very unique situation in the ruler Potiphar's home—basically serving as his second in command. However, Potiphar's wife was interested in more than conversation with him. As she began to pursue him and ask him to sleep with her, he responded in a way we should respond in that type of situation. Genesis 39:8–9 tells us, "Joseph refused. 'Look,' he told her, 'my master trusts me with everything in his entire household. No one here has more authority than I do. He has held back nothing from me except you, because you are his wife. How could I do such a wicked thing? It would be a great sin against God.'" Not only did Joseph understand he was blessed to be in the shoes he was in, he knew he would be sinning against God. Many times we try to figure out the dos and don'ts of dating, but that can be dangerous if we don't have the right goal in mind. Our goal should always be to see how much we can honor Christ in our relationship.

Boundaries shouldn't be set simply because a church leader said so, but because we value our walk with God and we want to help the other person guard their heart also, rather than take advantage of them. When Joseph informed Potiphar's wife that he wasn't going to do such a sinful thing, she didn't like that, but she knew exactly where he stood. I've learned that boundaries teach others what we will tolerate in our lives. The other person may not sign off on your decision, but that is not why we set boundaries—we do so to honor God rather than to receive others' approval. Joseph is a clear example of someone being selective in who he allowed into his life and who he allowed to experience parts of him that were meant only for a spouse.

It's important to value your time and your presence. Everyone doesn't deserve access to you. Our bodies were created to honor God, not to be a public playground.

> Boundaries teach others what we will tolerate in our lives.

Our hearts are meant to be valued, not simply tolerated or played with out of boredom. Don't be dismissive to others, but learn to be selective with who you allow to be close to you.

BOUNDARIES AROUND OUR BODIES

As we've discussed, we should all aim to guard our bodies. First Thessalonians 4:3–5 says this: "God's will is for you to be holy, so stay away from all sexual sin. Then each of you will control his own body and live in holiness and honor—not in lustful passion like the pagans who do not know God and his ways." What I (Safa) love about this passage of Scripture is that it plainly states that the will of God is for each of us believers to be holy, and that requires separation from sexual sin. We often question our ultimate purpose in life and what God desires for us to do here on this earth. These verses clearly tell us that God wants us to guard our bodies.

When it comes to establishing boundaries, we have to address things at the root. Every person isn't tempted by the same thing, so it is possible for these boundaries to be subjective and different for every believer. What I may consider normal, you may consider borderline sinful, and vice versa. To some, certain things aren't sins when dating: kissing, holding hands, long hugs, cuddling, or spending the night. While there isn't one Bible verse that says we should or shouldn't, I want you to ask yourself this: *Does this cause something to spark within me that shouldn't?*

Some things may not be sins, but can they lead to sin? While others can hug and cuddle all the time, I absolutely avoided that when dating. I have always been a physical touch person, so something simple could spark more for me. I didn't see it as a sin, but I knew it could usher sin into my life. Setting boundaries helped me prevent myself from going too far and allowing Tovares and me to stumble.

BOUNDARIES AROUND OUR EARS

One of the ways the Enemy crosses boundaries in our lives is through conversation. When we look at Genesis 3, we see how the serpent subtly crept his way into Eve's life through a conversation. When speaking with someone over time, we gradually become comfortable with them and allow their words to have some influence over us, both knowingly and unknowingly. That is what we see happening here with Eve in the garden of Eden. Eve was speaking with a very subtle serpent who got her to question God and His commands.

The conversation must have seemed innocent at first. He didn't come to her bashing God. He didn't come to her saying she was foolish for listening to God's commands. He simply pretended to care and got her to question what she believed. But not everyone who comes to you pretending to care actually has your best interests at heart. That is why discernment is needed in our lives.

When I (Tovares) told you how the military police checked our badges at the front gate of my naval base, you probably thought that's understandable. Maybe you live in a gated community yourself and have to use a special key fob just to get home. I've noticed that many of us are aware that we need to protect where we live, but how often do we forget to have boundaries about the voices speaking into our lives in conversation? We must properly filter the voices we listen to when trying to find direction on important decisions like who we date. We don't want to listen to a voice that causes us to compromise our walk with Jesus—the voice that tells us, "It doesn't take all that to be saved." That type of toxic voice in our lives will lead us down the path toward sin or complacency. It is imperative that we take the time to listen to a voice that is speaking what God desires for us. Because not all "good advice" is God's advice.

One story in the Bible illustrates that truth perfectly. In 1 Kings 13, God gave a prophet specific instructions to deliver a message to denounce King Jeroboam, and then go about his business. God informed the prophet that he shouldn't return to Judah the same way that he came. The only problem was, this prophet let his guard down when he ran into someone he thought he could trust. He ignored the king's request to come back to the palace for food and a gift because he knew God didn't want him getting comfortable there. But when he ran into an old prophet, he felt comfortable all of a sudden. The older man lied and said God had invited him back to where the prophet knew he shouldn't go. And he went. His mistake was feeling as though he could compromise on what God said due to the older prophet's position. We must be careful who we listen to because some connections can guide us away from our relationship with God.

I believe we use the term *friend* too loosely. Not everyone in close proximity to us is someone God desires for us to have in our lives. That young prophet was doing what God called him to—until he listened to that old, lying prophet. That story is a wake-up call to not entertain voices that tell us to do things contrary to the Word of God. True friends will not stop you from listening to and obeying what God has said.

BOUNDARIES AROUND OUR EYES

David was known as a man after God's own heart (Acts 13:22). Wow. What a way for God to label you. That's easily the biggest compliment He could've given to any of His children. David was a man full of passion. He wrote many psalms as a way to worship, cry out to God for help, and encourage others to serve the true God. He led the people to victory in so many battles. He remained humble and respectful to the preceding king, Saul, despite Saul's attempts to kill him. His résumé was easily the best in his time.

Despite all David's accomplishments and his passion for God, he still fell short of the glory of God. He loved God, but loving God love didn't prevent lust from creeping into his heart. He was a great king and leader, but that didn't exempt him from walking into sexual temptation.

We've talked about David and Bathsheba before, but let's explore the story from another angle. Instead of David going out to war with his troops the way he should have, he stayed back in Jerusalem. His poor decision put him in a place where he was looking at the wrong thing. It wasn't unusual for a king to be looking over the city while on a rooftop. The problem was that he noticed the beauty of Bathsheba as she bathed and he decided to not turn his head. Instead, he decided to inquire about a woman he shouldn't have been with.

We need boundaries around our eyes because we can't help what we notice, but we can determine what we are fixated on. Psalm 101:3 says: "I will set no wicked thing before mine eyes: I hate the work of them that turn aside; it shall not cleave to me" (KJV). Our bodies will always pursue what we continuously look at. We may not have control over what we see when walking the halls at school or browsing at the mall, but we have control over what we focus on. David couldn't make Bathsheba take her bath somewhere else, but he had the power to stop his eyes from focusing on her. He couldn't help her beauty, but he had the opportunity to be fighting at war with his men instead of taking a rest day.

The devil knew how to tempt Eve by appealing to her eyes. Genesis 3:4–6 tells us what happened:

> "You won't die!" the serpent replied to the woman. "God knows that your eyes will be opened as soon as you eat it, and you will be like God, knowing both good and evil." The woman was convinced. She saw that the tree was beautiful and its fruit looked delicious, and she wanted the wisdom it would give her. So she took some of the fruit and ate it. Then she gave some to her husband, who was with her, and he ate it, too.

As Eve continued her conversation with the serpent, he managed to show her how the fruit was pleasant to the eye. The tree didn't become more beautiful, but the tree became her focus. Eve knew God didn't want her eating from that tree, but after looking at it so much, it started to look desirable. I can only imagine how her conversation went with her husband. It appears that Adam simply said to avoid the tree altogether so they wouldn't disobey God. But the devil managed to get her to start staring at something that was off limits. If we don't guard our eyes, things that God tells us to avoid will begin to look appealing. Despite our knowing there are negative outcomes to sin, if we keep watching something that pulls us toward sin, eventually we will want more. The flesh is never satisfied. If our Enemy can get us looking the wrong way, he can get us to walk the wrong way.

I remember trying to overcome pornography but never seeming to get absolute freedom. It wasn't until I realized that I had to do more than turn off the XXX-rated shows. I had to delete the R-rated movies, even PG-13 sometimes, that weren't pornography but were still filled with perversion. I had to start filtering who I followed on social media. It might sound crazy and legalistic to some, but sometimes it's necessary to drastically cut some things out of our lives to have the kind of sober mind that is pleasing to Christ.

We often think we can control lust. That we can entertain just enough to have fun, but not enough for it to be harmful. That we're able to look, touch, and entertain certain things with our partner while not crossing the line. Unfortunately, sin will never be satisfied. If we open a door of opportunity to it, it will completely take over. It's like that one person who asks if they can spend the weekend with you while they sort out their living situation, but they're still with you six years later, comfortable and eating all the Frosted Flakes in your house.

BOUNDARIES HAVE TO BE CLEAR

I (Tovares) didn't run track and field very long as a child. I genuinely don't care to run unless something is chasing me. But track shows us something that we could easily overlook. Every runner has a couple of lines he or she must stick to. If you cross those lines, or boundaries, into the next lane, you not only run the risk of disqualification, but you might also harm yourself and other runners. When people think of injuries in track, we can easily envision a pulled hamstring or someone rolling their ankle by landing on it improperly. Few of us understand that all it takes is for one person to step into our lane, and then there can be a collision of two or three people, depending on how close you are. You've got to stay in your lane.

The thing about boundaries is that they clearly show others what we are willing to tolerate. When Safa and I were dating, we had to come up with a list of things we wouldn't do so we could guard ourselves from allowing our flesh to take over. We created a list on our Notes app to share between us, so we could constantly be reminded of the convictions we wanted to abide by. Because I'm a visual person, I knew I had to make it clear that we shouldn't change in front of one another or get on FaceTime dressed provocatively. I'm not guaranteeing that secular music is going to make any of you stumble, but we needed to make it clear that we couldn't be listening to music together that was made to set the mood for activities we were trying to save for marriage. We told each other our expectations regarding communication; we made it clear that we wouldn't allow anger or our egos to cause us to speak in a condescending manner to one another, and we also wouldn't allow flirting to get to a point where it would spark something else.

When we made this list, we had every intention of following it, but that didn't always happen. Sometimes I didn't want to do the very things that I recommended, but that's because our human nature normally chooses its own desires more than God's will. When the devil tempted Eve, he made her think that disobeying God would be pleasurable. But boundaries are not to restrict us; they are meant to protect us. Proverbs 25:28 shows us a vivid example of what a person without self-control is like. It reads, "A person without self-control is like a city with broken-down walls." A city without walls is a city anyone can trespass into and impose their will. When we set clear boundaries, we allow ourselves and others to avoid pain, heartache, and sin.

Have you made your boundaries clear in your life? What about in your relationship? Have you informed your significant other that you aren't going to settle for abusive language or a lukewarm foundation? Are you assuming they shouldn't expect sex because you love Jesus, or did you tell them it was nonnegotiable? It's wise to mention things you want to avoid because they can be a trigger for you. If they respect and value you, they will honor those guidelines. When you verbalize these boundaries, you can create a meaningful and lasting relationship, because you are making it clear to the other person what you desire and what you will not tolerate. Then you can avoid getting frustrated or resentful, because they will know what is expected if they want to be a part of your life.

People will continuously aim to create a standard for you if your standards aren't previously established. We have been pushing boundaries since the garden of Eden, and someone is probably pushing their limits with us now. It might be through your inbox, or with a toddler like ours who's building our patience. When it comes to the limits in your life, don't let someone else create them for you. The only thing that should influence your boundaries is the Word of God, not culture. The safest place to find direction is the Word of God. Psalm 119:105 says this about the Word: "Your word is a lamp to guide my feet and a light for my path." Society has a new standard for sexuality and relationships every couple of years. If we allow our relationships to be driven by what Hollywood is doing, we won't experience the true joy that is only found in Christ. We have to follow His Word and allow Him to be our guide, because nothing good comes from a relationship that lacks boundaries.

A lack of boundaries may cause us to think we are truly living our best life and are on our road to freedom, but this may actually be leading us to sin or more unnecessary drama, battles, and pain.

God has anointed all His children to do His will, and I am sure He is able to complete the work He started in each of us (Philippians 1:6). However, many of us are living beneath the standard He has for us because we haven't established boundaries. Remember, David was a man after God's own heart, but a lack of boundaries led to him making decisions with Bathsheba that he shouldn't have. Solomon was a wise man who made poor decisions due to not having boundaries in the types of women he decided to marry. We don't have to repeat those cycles anymore.

We can choose to create our own personal boundaries today—boundaries that protect our spiritual growth and won't pull us away from prayer, fasting, and studying the Word. Boundaries that won't allow us to listen to gossip or those who like to slander others. Boundaries that cause us to walk away from a relationship instead of allowing that relationship to pull us away from our commitment to what God has planned for us. Boundaries in a relationship that help protect our purity and theirs instead of allowing hormones to guide us. A lack of boundaries does more than harm you; we do a disservice to future generations when we choose what's convenient now over what God has for us. People with true wisdom know this: life is better with boundaries.

GODSENT OR COUNTERFEIT?

I (Tovares) found a nice local barbershop in my city that only accepted cash. I'm the type of person who rarely walks around with cash; I only have my card on me. So whenever I'm going for a haircut, I'll either go to a nearby ATM or a local grocery store and withdraw money at checkout.

This time I went to a nearby Publix and withdrew twenty dollars for my haircut. I took that same twenty dollars and handed it to my barber as I was walking out. The very next day my wife took our son, Zion, there to get his hair cut. They told her to have me call them when I got the chance, but they didn't tell her why. I was very confused to hear that. If I'd forgotten my wallet there overnight, they would have given it to her.

I called the barber and asked what was wrong. He explained that I had paid him with a fake twenty-dollar bill! I was completely discombobulated. Was he trying to be funny? Did someone else pay him with a counterfeit bill and he confused the two? Surely this must be a prank for his secret TikTok account. I asked him if he was joking, and he insisted that it really was fake money. He said he kept the money to give it back when I got there. I decided to take care of it myself rather than burdening Safa with such a crazy story. Sure enough, when I went back to him, he had a counterfeit bill to hand to me! I couldn't help but laugh that I was the person to end up with fake money. So I just paid him for the haircut and we moved on.

Looking back, I still wish I could have avoided that encounter. It could have been avoided if I noticed the counterfeit money when I received it from the grocery store. When I withdrew the money, I didn't inspect it for any discrepancies or judge it by other twenties I've held in the past. I simply trusted that I wouldn't ever make a mistake like that. I hadn't had this issue before, so I didn't expect to ever have to deal with it.

I believe this is a problem many of us have in our spiritual lives as well. Not that you don't know the difference between fake or authentic money, but you probably don't take the time to examine things, like I failed to do that day. We see something that looks authentic or real, but we don't realize it's just a matter of outside appearance. Without proper inspection, we can casually connect to a beautiful distraction. As much as I would love to believe that everyone in church actually loves Jesus, I would be fooling myself to think that. It's reckless to simply connect to someone and call them "God's will" for our lives just because they have "man of God" in their social media bio.

I can attest that most women I had ungodly connections with considered themselves "Proverbs 31 women." (Remember that chapter in Proverbs describes a woman who was hard working, God fearing, loving, and a blessing to her family.) I don't say this to shame other women, because I was beyond lukewarm at times and far from the biblical ideal. I've just learned that it's not enough to take the label and leave the lifestyle. It's possible to appear spiritual, but have our hearts be anything but rooted in the Word of God.

One thing we must grasp about our Enemy is that he normally sends counterfeits that appear to meet our preferences. Every person is tempted when they are enticed by things their heart desires (James 1:14). The Enemy is carefully studying us. If you like them tall, dark, and handsome, he won't send you short, pale, and ugly. If you like them curvy, curly-haired, and Latina, he isn't sending slim, straight-haired, and European. If he did, you'd immediately start rebuking the devil. But few of us can see a distraction when it fits the description that we are in love with. Remember, the Bible makes it clear that our Enemy will disguise himself as an angel of light in an effort to deceive us (2 Corinthians 11:14). It's possible that everything we desire in a spouse outwardly will be presented to us in the form of a relationship that God didn't ordain. That's how deception works. The Enemy will show us something that looks appealing and authentic but in reality is fake. A man may preach the greatest sermon, but his life outside of the pulpit may be abusive. A woman may have the most modest wardrobe and speak fluent King James Version, but her flattering words can lead straight to hell (Proverbs 5:3–5). If we are honest, that may have been some of us before God began to cleanse and sanctify us. Because God is aiming to change who we are, not just how we look.

As we discussed earlier, it is possible for someone to attend church but not truly live for Christ. I know it's possible because that used to be me. Someone may attend every service. They might be a part of a small group. They may even pay a tithe from every paycheck! Nevertheless, they could be doing all those things for show and not out of a genuine love for Jesus. Speaking in tongues is great, but it doesn't take away the fact that God desires for our lives to have integrity, character, and the fruit of the Spirit (Galatians 5:22–23). There can be big differences between those who attend church and those actually living for Christ.

GODLY PERSON VS. CHURCHGOER

The people we see in church may or may not be saved, so you shouldn't be dating or marrying just anyone from church. You aren't compatible with everyone just because they are a believer, and everyone in the house of God isn't living a life that is honoring Christ. There have been times in my life when I know I was guilty of being faithful to the building but not faithful to His Word. That led to me becoming a negative influence on women as well.

When I think of people who are in church but aren't in a

relationship with Jesus, I think of Judas. So many people complain about their pastors, but Judas literally had the best pastor to walk this earth. I mean, how do you compete with God in the flesh? I'm sure Jesus' church was better than mine. But Judas walked with Jesus daily and wasn't fully converted. He saw things that many of us haven't—the healings, the demons being cast out, the feeding of thousands, walking on water, lives being set free from darkness, and more. I'm getting jealous just thinking about those great opportunities. After seeing all those things, his heart still chose money over Jesus. He betrayed the Son of God for temporary gain. Now, before we get on our high horses, please understand we've all betrayed Jesus at some point when we've sinned instead of obeying Him.

Judas was right next to Jesus and still didn't live the way he should have. If he could miss the mark, I know the same can happen for us. That's why we don't pursue a spouse based on their church attendance, but their lifestyle. Neither should we think we are pleasing God because of how often we pop up for Sunday school. Jesus said if we love Him, we will obey His Word (John 14:15). Our obedience to God and love for others will determine if we are following Jesus or simply attending service. It's time to pay attention to fruit more than looks.

BE GOOD-FRUIT INSPECTORS

There are times when I (Safa) have purchased fruit at the store that looked fresh, like it could last for at least a week. When it comes to fruits and vegetables, I try to stay in the organic section because those are expected to be the healthiest. I know that if I buy my fruit from certain produce stores, I should have no issue with quality—or so I thought. On some occasions, within a day or two I'm left with regret when I try to make my strawberry banana smoothie and see that three of my strawberries have mold on them. You'd think that I would've noticed that at the store. However, I just glanced at the surface level and assumed they were all in good condition because they were organic. I didn't see the few areas hinting toward a gradual growth of mold. I just assumed that since it was Publix, the best grocery store in Florida, I should be fine. Strike two, Publix!

As you read this book, I'm calling you to become a fruit inspector. Sis, I am sure when that handsome man approaches you, your heart may skip a beat because he noticed you in the crowd of other women. But beyond his charm and good looks, I want you to see the fruit his life is bearing. He may find you attractive, but that doesn't mean God sent him. And to all my brothers reading, I want you to find that woman you are attracted to, but before you choose her because of her curves and pretty smile, I encourage you to see if she's passionate about her walk with Christ. We have to start evaluating the person before we connect to them. We have to see the fruit of the Holy Spirit as outlined in Galatians 5 before we start planning our future with them.

Trust me, I get it. Many of you reading this may cringe at the thought of "judging" someone else's walk with God. You don't want to come across as self-righteous or belittle anyone who may have issues with sin in their personal life. However, we have to understand that the Bible is very clear when it says to guard our hearts (Proverbs 4:23). What we allow into our hearts and minds will influence the direction we are headed. If we choose to leave our hearts vulnerable, without proper protection, we allow rotten apples into our lives who can spread their dysfunction. Mold doesn't spread to other fruit unless it's in close proximity. That's why Paul said that bad company will corrupt good character (1 Corinthians 15:33). We're not asking you to question someone's salvation, but we are asking you to question if that person is helping or hindering your walk with Jesus. God calls us to love and respect everyone, but He didn't tell us we should open our hearts to people who may be destructive to our purpose. Again, entertaining relationships God didn't ordain can lead to us walking outside of God's will (Psalm 106:34).

I know many of us would like to simply date someone in church and just assume that things couldn't go bad or lead into sin. Unfortunately, that's just not the case. It is very easy to undergo a lot of emotional abuse and frustration even from someone who is in church. They may even serve in ministry and still not have the type of character and spiritual fruit that God desires us believers to produce. Examining fruit is essential because you want to be sure your future marriage can honor God and your children will grow in the fear of the Lord. Settling for someone who doesn't have that same desire to live for God won't lead to a fulfilling marriage as God intends.

We want you to be able to spot some differences between a man or a woman who looks the part and the one who can actually help you grow into who God destined you to be. The one you can find a relationship with that doesn't lead straight to sex but leads to marriage first. Someone who will help you stay in the will of God instead of distracting you from Him. Who won't criticize your devotion and praise like Job's or David's wives did but will encourage and support you. Someone who is exhibiting the fruit of the Spirit in their lives. We can easily say, "Wait on a genuine woman/man of God," but that's not always as easy as it sounds. Why? Many of us don't realize the difference between someone who is godly and someone who simply calls themselves a believer. We know someone is godly not because of their words, but because we see them exhibiting love, joy, peace, patience, kindness, goodness, faithfulness, gentleness, and self-control in their actions. First, let's discuss what a counterfeit is and a few signs that help to identify one.

HOW TO IDENTIFY THE COUNTERFEIT

If we can't see when someone isn't sent by God, we can easily lose our focus on what God is trying to do in our lives. When you think of a counterfeit, you may think of something that isn't real. However, a counterfeit will always look real, smell real, and have almost every feature you may desire. Without proper examination, you can mistakenly accept it as real, just like I (Tovares) did with my fake twenty-dollar bill. We often think an ungodly relationship is one that makes us renounce Christ and curse out our friends, or one that is abusive. But you know it isn't God's will if you experience a drift away from the direction God is aiming to take you, no matter the person's position in church and how often they are leading Bible study. Now I want us to explore ways to spot when someone isn't sent by God into our lives.

THEY ARE LEADING YOU CLOSER TO SIN.

Almost everyone considers themselves "spiritual" in the world today. Many claim Christ in their social media bios. It's trendy to wear the Jesus chain and even post the Sunday morning selfies holding their Bible and Starbucks coffee. But it seems like everyone is a Christian until things get biblical. As we strive to get closer to Jesus, we must cease making excuses for those who encourage us to disobey what God said.

If the Bible tells you to run away from sexual immorality, a godly person shouldn't pressure you into sex before marriage. If the Bible encourages you to avoid things that lead you to sin, they shouldn't encourage you to rebel against what the Bible says. Better yet, if the Bible says something is a sin, they shouldn't try to justify it and find reasons to explain to you why it's perfectly okay and the Bible is outdated. I don't aim to trigger anyone by saying this, but I believe it's necessary to actually take the Bible seriously. Our generation needs to get back to fearing God rather than allowing our vile culture to redefine Christianity.

Proverbs 1:10 puts it this way: "My son, if sinners entice

you, do not consent" (ESV). If you don't believe anything else I'm telling you, believe this: God loves you too much to send you someone who will pull you into sin. God desires a relationship with each of us, and He wants to spend time with us. Someone who wants to lead you away from His will is a distraction. They may be your type, but some distractions can be attractive.

Ladies, if a man isn't leading you closer to Jesus, he isn't ready to lead a home spiritually. Men, if a woman won't submit to Christ for herself, she won't submit to a husband who is submitted to Him. A clear red flag is when someone is not taking their spiritual life seriously. That is an indicator that they won't care about your growth either. This person can't make you better if they minimize your walk with Jesus.

THEY CAUSE YOU TO QUESTION AND LET GO OF YOUR BIBLICAL CONVICTIONS.

Growing up, I (Tovares) didn't question all the rules in my house because I understood why my parents said what they said. I didn't question the rules at school because I knew how often we gave the teachers a hard time. Neither did I question the rules in the navy, because I knew they were in place to maintain good order and discipline. But when it came to church, I saw a much different perspective. I noticed many people in local churches complained about everything the church leadership would say. They complied everywhere else, but listening to leadership in church always made them say they wanted to be free from "bondage."

I won't even lie to you. I really had my days when I felt the church had too many rules or expectations for us. But most of my questions stemmed from the voices I was listening to. I assumed a person was hearing from God because they looked spiritual. I assumed they were helping me get closer to Jesus simply because they wore a suit or a long skirt. So if someone I assumed was spiritual began to rebel or negatively criticize leaders, I assumed it had to be normal. I believe that this is where Eve fell into sin. Not because she didn't love God, but because she connected to someone who didn't care about her connection to Him.

Have you ever heard someone ask these questions?

- Did God really say that?
- Does God really need you in church so much?
- Does God really have a problem if we have sex just once?
- Is a loving God going to actually send you to hell if we do this?

That list can go on and on, but the results will be the same. A counterfeit will always try to question what God said rather than help you obey and follow His Word. We're not talking about someone who is blatantly atheist or someone who loathes the church. Many of these types of people we're talking about are in the church. They simply mask their approach with concern. They disguise their rebellion with a spiritual facade. That is why you must check if their fruit is causing you to walk away from Jesus, instead of drawing you closer to Him.

HOW TO IDENTIFY THE GODSENT

Now that you know how to spot a counterfeit, here are a few things you can recognize as good signs that the person you're considering is the real deal.

THEY ARE BUILDING THEIR OWN WALK WITH GOD.

Sometimes someone doesn't mind you growing, but they won't be intentional in their spiritual walk. Psalm 34:8 says, "O taste and see that the LORD is good: blessed is the man that trusteth in him" (KJV). The moment you see someone spending time with Jesus in order to grow, not to date you, you know they value the presence of God in their lives. It's not enough to know that God is good; they should desire to experience that goodness for themselves. We all must encounter the presence and love of Jesus for ourselves and not simply fabricate an unauthentic spiritual life simply to impress others.

I (Tovares) am thankful that when God allowed me to meet Safa, I never had to question her spiritual life. I never wondered if she would be a spiritual hindrance to my purpose. I never questioned if she was spiritually mature enough to date, because I saw the fruit she produced and her faithfulness to the things of God. I was sure that she was worth marrying because I saw that she loved God more than anything else. I loved how I could see how gentle, patient, and loving she was. Her lifestyle was proof that she both loved people and had a heart focused on pleasing God.

Someone who is building their own walk with God is less likely to compromise to please others. They are willing to help you get closer to Jesus and your purpose. It's not enough for us believers to simply "avoid sin." I believe God wants us to stay connected to people who are seeking Him with pure hearts. Second Timothy 2:22 tells us we should "run from anything that stimulates youthful lusts. Instead, pursue righteous living, faithfulness, love, and peace. Enjoy the companionship of those who call on the Lord with pure hearts." A life of purity becomes easier as we stay connected to those who have the same desire to follow Jesus.

THEY RESPECT YOUR BOUNDARIES.

We believe it is the will of God for His children to only date someone who will respect their biblical convictions. God's Word explicitly shows us how sex outside of marriage isn't honoring God or beneficial to our relationship, so it is wise for us to wait on someone who is willing to encourage us along our path of purity. Remember, 1 Corinthians 15:33 says, "Don't be fooled by those who say such things, for 'bad company corrupts good character.'"

Let's take a moment and be honest with ourselves here. When interested in someone, it is very easy to push the limits or to let your guard down simply because you're comfortable. When you have someone who respects your boundaries, you know that they value more than your purity. They are showing you they also value their walk with God.

Solomon warns us to not consent if someone is aiming to

lead us into sin (Proverbs 1:10). If you give the devil an inch in your life, he will take a mile. Discernment is key because we want God to show us who is aiming to invest in us and who will simply take from us. Remember, boyfriends and girlfriends don't get spouse privileges.

GOD HAS GIVEN YOU PEACE ABOUT IT.

When God is behind a decision, He will always give us His peace. Some decisions in life always seem scary initially, whether it's starting a new job, switching schools, or beginning a relationship. But when you're walking in God's will and building your walk with Him, He will guide your steps. As He guides us, we know that He wants to bless us. The Bible literally says that God won't withhold a good thing from us as we walk uprightly (Psalm 84:11). That's proof to us that He won't send a relationship that brings confusion.

Paul told the church in Corinth that God is not the author of confusion (1 Corinthians 14:33). That reassures me that God's will does not bring dysfunction or disorder. Read that again. Remind yourself of that the next time you're questioning if God desires someone in your life. It's not that a godly relationship won't experience problems, but it shouldn't have you wrestling daily with uncertainty. You should have peace knowing that this relationship is honoring God—peace knowing that in moments of weakness, God blessed you with someone who can pray for you rather than prey on you. You'll have peace knowing that if you have a family together, you have someone who can teach your children the truth about God and His Word.

If you see that you're constantly conflicted, maybe God wasn't behind that relationship. Just because we desire something doesn't mean that God was behind it. We have to be careful to not allow our desires to become our guide, because it's always better to follow His will instead of our emotions. That will help us distinguish between what is Godsent and what is counterfeit.

8

LET IT GO

I (Tovares) grew up in a house full of athletes.
My dad played soccer and my mom ran track. So naturally, all
their boys did some form of sports. We all ran track, but I didn't
care too much for competing because I'm just not fast like my
brothers were. Football was my passion. Even though I couldn't
run fast on the track, I still loved to watch my brothers race.
When I think of an athlete running a race, immediately my
mind visualizes track and field and the fast athletes we have
in this world: the famous American athletes like Allyson Felix
or the legendary Carl Lewis. Record-shattering stars like Usain
Bolt, who electrified the crowd every time he stepped foot on the
track. Being that Safa and I are both of Jamaican descent (Safa
was actually born there), you can guarantee that we are proud
onlookers every time the Olympics come on. We were confident

Usain Bolt would win, yet eager to watch him make our island proud. The real competition was always over who would have to claim the silver and bronze.

Despite the speed of these sprinters, it is possible that ordinary people like you and I could beat Olympic runners in a foot race. I know that sounds crazy, but it is possible. If the fastest athlete in the world decided to run against me while he was wearing jeans, boots, a backpack, and pushing a double stroller, I might have a chance. You might say, "That's absurd. Why would someone race with all that baggage?" It seems unreasonable for someone aiming to win a race to decide to grab more baggage that would slow down their chance at victory. But that is what you and I look like when we decide to run this Christian race and carry unnecessary baggage that God wants us to cast on Him (1 Peter 5:7)—to pick up things that aren't helping us reach our ultimate goal, Jesus.

When you observe a track meet, notice that the athletes are not wearing much clothing. It's not that their aim is to be immodest, but they are aware that they have to be freer in order to go farther and faster. I remember days when I would have to run while at work in the military. Maybe something was wrong with a patient or I was out in the field with the marines. We still got to our destination, just not at the fastest pace while dressed in uniform. When it came to the physical readiness test, or PRT, we were allowed to wear light fitness clothing. We were expected to do a certain number of push-ups and sit-ups and run a certain distance within a certain time in order to pass. If we tried it in uniform, we would have easily had many failures. It's not that we don't have a "right" to run in certain clothing, but some things are unhelpful. Running this Christian race is similar. We always have things weighing us down that God is calling us to release. Hebrews 12:1 shows us that we should lay aside the sins and the weights in our lives. In other words, some things in our lives may not be considered "sin," but they can slow us down if we choose to hold on to them.

Whether we aim to believe it or not, unforgiveness has an irrational hold on countless believers in the church today. Many of us are unable to find a healthy relationship, because our previous one hurt us drastically and we are still hanging on to those hurts. Some of us push away everyone God sends our way because a friend betrayed us. Or maybe you are always skeptical about the pastor because you had a manipulative leader before. Maybe you never go home for Thanksgiving, because you have so many childhood memories that haunt you to this day. But what if you didn't have to walk in bondage to bitterness? What if it's actually God's will for you to have peace instead of resentment? It's really God's will that you have a garment of joy instead of a spirit of heaviness (Isaiah 61:3).

WHAT IS FORGIVENESS?

To forgive is to release someone from a debt that they owe. Relationally speaking, it's choosing to not retaliate when someone does something that upsets or provokes us. To forgive someone is to not allow what hurt you to continue to haunt you, choosing instead to be free. Despite all the power in His hands, Jesus didn't get down off the cross or fight back when the people aimed to criticize or crucify Him because he was extending forgiveness for their despicable actions (Luke 23:34). Forgiveness is not pretending it didn't happen. Concealing your wounds and expecting to overcome the agony by masking it is simply being unrealistic and is harmful to your emotional and psychological well-being. The person who wronged you may deserve every bit of retaliation you may want to inflict on them. Without a doubt, getting even may bring temporary relief to our flesh, but seeking retribution isn't what God desires from us. To forgive someone means that despite remembering what happened, you don't allow your emotions to become imprisoned to the past (Romans 12:17–21). Allow God to handle the vengeance, and choose to not allow the sting of someone else's actions to haunt you further.

I have seen some misconceptions about forgiveness infiltrate the church. It's important that we get the right idea of forgiveness in mind, so we can move forward with hearts that aren't cold or calloused toward God or people in this world. Proverbs 18:19 says, "An offended friend is harder to win back than a fortified city. Arguments separate friends like a gate locked with bars." Unforgiveness shuts others out and causes us to build walls that can separate us from the very people God wants in our lives. Society doesn't mind your harboring animosity, but we are stronger together. There is no true peace when we hold grudges, so it's time to release the indignation that has been lurking in the corners of our hearts.

DON'T WAIT UNTIL YOU FEEL LIKE IT

First and foremost, forgiveness isn't a feeling; it's a choice. Some days you won't think you have the capacity to forgive. You'll have to muster up the courage to even face certain individuals who may have wounded you. However, forgiveness shouldn't depend on how you are feeling. If I only did my work when I felt like it, I would fail my class or risk being fired. If you allowed a child to only shower or brush their teeth when they felt like it, you would have a house full of smelly children. Our feelings may be valid, but they are terrible guides. That's why it's so important to remember what Jeremiah 17:9 tells us: "The human heart is the most deceitful of all things, and desperately wicked. Who really knows how bad it is?" Our hearts will deceive us into thinking we can simply forgive someone when we feel like it, but God expects us to forgive despite how we feel (Matthew 6:14–15). We know that when God forgives us, we might not physically or emotionally feel like anything happened, but God is greater than our hearts and emotions (1 John 3:20). We have to determine that we will forgive despite our mood—that we will live like Jesus no matter how someone decided to treat us. Their actions shouldn't determine our commitment to obeying the Word of God.

Furthermore, forgiveness is not synonymous with reconciliation. It is imperative that we are aware of our need for proper boundaries after someone constantly antagonizes us and violates our trust. People assume that because Jesus expects us to forgive, He wants us to remain friends or in relationships with everyone. This misinterpretation is why people have difficulty forgiving.

They have examined the fruit of this person's lifestyle, so they are afraid of letting their guard down and letting the cycle continue. On the contrary, some people we must forgive but avoid thereafter. Not because we're banishing them to hell or because they no longer deserve grace, but because we choose to protect our hearts and minds from their abuse and dysfunction. Trust should develop over time. Don't force relationships that God may be removing you from. Now, they may feel disrespected that you would implement limits to their access into your life, but you can't allow manipulation to pull you back to that cycle God just freed you from. Mistakes that are constantly repeated are no longer mistakes, but choices. Patterns shouldn't be ignored. If you are in an abusive relationship currently, that isn't what God desires for you. He wants you to forgive for the pain inflicted, but He isn't calling you to stay with that person and become a punching bag. Emotional and physical abuse are still prevalent in our world today, but you have to be willing to forgive in order to move forward.

Another fallacy I've stumbled upon is that if someone breaks your heart, you can simply find someone new to heal your heart. *Just get a new man who will treat you right. Find the woman who won't cheat this time.* Unfortunately, mankind can't heal you, no matter how attractive or charming a person is. We all are imperfect beings who sin. Our sinful nature causes us to offend people when we didn't even intend to. Healing and wholeness can be found only in Christ, not a new relationship. Colossians 2:9–10 says, "In Christ lives all the fullness of God in a human body. So you also are complete through your union with Christ, who is the head over every ruler and authority." That means no one else can complete you.

We need to heal from our past before God opens the next door. If we can't forgive our ex and release the baggage, why should God send someone else? When we hold on to unforgiveness, we carry it into the next relationship. Emotions left unchecked and insecurities left unaddressed will always arise there. Instead of making your next relationship pay for the harm your ex inflicted, it's time to forgive, so you can create something that isn't tainted with the stains of your past. Forgiving is necessary before you can find someone new; if you think joy and peace will come from a new relationship, that person will quickly become an idol. You will turn a blessing into something that will eventually become a curse.

Forgiveness is hard because many of us have the wrong view of God. When we start viewing God in all His holiness and beauty, we will see why forgiveness isn't just a necessity for those who have proven they're worthy of it. Instead, we will see that forgiveness is actually a way of life. We must learn that forgiveness is necessary to have an authentic walk with Jesus.

GOD IS NOT LIKE US

Some of us have a special gift that isn't a fruit of the Spirit, and that's the ability to be petty. If you don't know what that is, that simply means that we are either ungenerous or mean regarding something that is insignificant. There's no need for sarcasm, but we dish it out anyway. We don't have to be upset about the fifty cents someone owed us from the third grade, but we are still upset about it. The moment they post a Starbucks picture on Facebook, we are ready to give them a piece of our mind for not paying us before buying that Caramel Frappuccino.

One of the most liberating things I (Tovares) have learned about God is that He is not like us. Personally, I'm relieved that God doesn't have a flawed character like us humans. In the past, I have made some people so upset that they decided to never speak to me again. And to be honest, I can hold a grudge too. Many of us have grieved the heart of God with our sin, rebellion, or inconsistent spiritual life, but He has never dismissed us the way others can. Psalm 103:8 says, "The LORD is compassionate and merciful, slow to get angry and filled with unfailing love."

God is always willing to forgive us when we repent. Second Corinthians 5:19 informs us that "God was in Christ, reconciling the world to himself, no longer counting people's sins against them. And he gave us this wonderful message of reconciliation." Not only is it God's aim to forgive you, He wants us to forgive others in the same manner we have been forgiven—a message of reconciliation. Heaven doesn't endorse cancel culture; God desires to see people forgiven and restored.

HEALING IS A PROCESS

Have you ever heard the saying that "time heals all wounds"? That proverb has been popular for years, but it still isn't necessarily true. It is possible that you're reading this and still haven't forgiven your ex for how the last relationship ended. Many people are dealing with the aftermath of childhood abuse while they are currently deep into their thirties (or forties, or fifties). Just because years go by doesn't mean we can simply "get over" the fact that we were bullied, harassed, rejected, neglected, or worse. The idea that you'll get over the heartache with just a little time isn't necessarily true. This mentality has taught us that it's okay to suppress our feelings rather than allow God to heal them. We sometimes ignore our pain instead of allowing God to heal us in His presence. The abuse you endured shouldn't be ignored. Letting time erase memories doesn't mean your spirit has been healed. Forgiveness doesn't mean forgetting. We know we have forgiven someone when even if we do remember what happened and how it made us feel, we decide we will not allow the past to imprison us—that the person who harmed us will not cause us to walk in bitterness and hatred any longer.

Time can pass and wounds will still remain, depending on the severity of the issue. We need to do more than simply let the clock run; we must be intentional in allowing God to remove the heavy burden of our pain and our grief. I believe the old saying is better off with some changes: "God heals all wounds in time." In the presence of God, we find fullness of joy (Psalm 16:11). It's possible that society is telling you to let time pass, but what you may need is more time in God's presence. Prayer and the Word of God are the best gifts given to believers, yet the most underutilized. We should seek God until we are completely healed from the past. We must ask God to give us the strength and the grace to forgive others how He has forgiven us. When we enter back into God's presence through spiritual intimacy, we see who He truly is. And when we have a revelation of who Jesus is, He will show us our true identity again (Matthew 16:16–18). One thing we must understand about healing is that the process is different for everyone. Depending on the level of hurt, some things may take more time to overcome. But we all can rest assured that God is able to heal any wound we've experienced (Isaiah 61:1).

In the past, I thought I needed to find closure in order to find healing. Now I've learned that healing is personal, between you and God. It's something we choose, with or without an apology. Some people will offend us and then play the victim role. Closure is highly overrated and not always feasible. Some of us are firmly holding on to pain from a death or a loss, or from people who have dumped us, gotten married, and are now on their third child. Some of us are mad at someone living in a whole other state. If we believe it's necessary to speak to them personally before we forgive, we're overcomplicating things. We must learn to forgive and release the pain for the sake of our healing. Forgiveness isn't always a one-time event, but an ongoing process we have to commit to instead of allowing the negative history to hinder the future God has for us. If possible, it is important for you to seek out those you may have offended. Jesus taught us that if we remember someone with something against us, we should pause our worship and seek forgiveness and reconciliation before offering our gift to God (Matthew 5:23–24). We can only do what depends on us. Rather than just letting time go by or letting the idea of "closure" call the shots, we must turn to God first.

EVEN WHEN IT HURTS

I (Safa) don't like to allow trivial issues to faze me. I consider myself a very laid-back person who can overlook much before letting anger or bitterness kick in. I've always believed that someone else's actions aren't a reflection of my character, but rather a reflection of their own and the mindset they possess. But there was a time when my character was challenged, and I had to learn to forgive something I never thought I would ever have to forgive.

In the early stages of our marriage, while using Tovares' laptop, I stumbled upon distasteful conversations between him and other women who lacked boundaries. I had just had our first child, and I was vulnerable and deficient in confidence in myself because I looked and felt different. I was struggling to rediscover who I was in the midst of all the new changes in my life. It couldn't have been a worse time for me to accidentally find out he was struggling with lust. My heart was broken, to say the least. Not because of his imperfection, because I understood that everyone struggles with something, but because I had to find out the way I did. I felt he could have told me because he knew I wouldn't have judged him or lashed out. I still would have been hurt, but more than anything, I would have wanted to be there to help him overcome this thorn in his flesh. That's what a wife is for.

The fact that I felt he didn't trust me enough to open up about such a delicate issue he was dealing with made me feel we weren't as close as I thought we were, and it made me wonder what else he might be hiding. That's where the hurt stemmed from the most. I wanted to lash out because I no longer trusted him, knowing that he had been keeping something like that from me. I didn't want to speak to him. I didn't want to forgive him. And I felt I was justified in my reasoning. But with all the reasons I've given God not to forgive me, He still had, and He is still forgiving me daily. I couldn't live in my bitterness. I learned to forgive him, and I learned over time to trust him again.

I understand many of you reading this might not be married yet, and forgiveness in your dating or other relationships might look a little different. By God's standards, yes, you are still expected to forgive them, but you forgive someone in order to have peace within yourself. Extending forgiveness doesn't mean we are planning to overlook the actions that lead to distrust. We cannot just blame the devil alone and not allow the other person to assume responsibility for their actions. They should still have to own up to their mistakes.

WHY FORGIVE?

The truth of God's Word says, "Be kind and compassionate to one another, forgiving one another, just as God also forgave you in Christ" (Ephesians 4:32 csb). Over time, I truly had to ask God to help me heal. God had to teach me to forgive what I couldn't forget. To show me what it means to love my husband in the way that God loves me every single day. Why? Because Jesus never died for me because of how good I was. In reality, nobody is good. We tend to harbor resentment toward people who frustrate us, but imagine if God did that. No person can offend us to the level that our sin offends God. Yet, He forgave us and gave us a chance at eternal life before we were even walking in His will. Romans 5:8 tells us, "God showed his great love for us by sending Christ to die for us while we were still sinners." We find what true love is when we look at the story of Jesus. How He was willing to step down in the middle of mess and to love us despite it all. To cleanse us and to get us back on the path toward God. I don't believe it's the will of God that we run back to every ex that we've had, but I believe many relationships fail because we choose to hold on to unforgiveness. There is no excuse for betrayal, just like there is no excuse for us choosing sin. But if God can restore a sinner, we have to learn to forgive things that we didn't see coming as well.

When people dream of godly relationships, sometimes they get the impression that the two of you will be so perfect that you'll never experience a storm, that your heart will never experience pain, and that you won't have to argue. None of that is biblical. There hasn't been a day when we have regretted marriage due to our conflicts, because conflicts are simply opportunities to grow closer to God and to each another.

IS THIS A HEAVEN-OR-HELL ISSUE?

Many of us are confident in our salvation, but not because of our good works. We all can boldly declare like Paul that Christ came to save sinners, and we are probably the worst of them all

(1 Timothy 1:15). I (Tovares) can tell you that if Paul would've seen my list, I'm sure he would let me hold that title. But we still know we have no need to question our salvation. Through our faith, God has forgiven us of our sins (John 3:16; Acts 2:38; Ephesians 2:8). However, there is a point in Scripture when we read that God won't forgive us: "If you forgive those who sin against you, your heavenly Father will forgive you. But if you refuse to forgive others, your Father will not forgive your sins" (Matthew 6:14–15).

Without forgiveness of sins, none of us will see our heavenly Father in the life to come. Now some of you may be wondering if I just condemned everyone to hell who hasn't exemplified forgiveness in every encounter with wrongdoing. "So you're saying that if you don't forgive your ex you're heading toward hell?" No, I don't believe so. Thankfully, God isn't like us. We don't have to worry about Him being immature and waiting on opportunities to take salvation back. I just want us to grasp the gravity of the words of Jesus. You cannot expect forgiveness from God if you won't share it with those who hurt you. When tempted to harbor unforgiveness, we should ask God to jog our memory. We should recall the sacrifice He paid at Calvary, knowing some would reject Him and still not believe.

You may still somehow reach heaven while maintaining bitterness and unforgiveness in your heart, but you will have to carry unnecessary baggage from choosing to not forgive today. Unconfessed sin in our hearts will hinder our prayers from being heard or answered (Psalm 66:18). Unforgiveness will lead to us insecurities and trust issues that we shouldn't have to deal with.

Unforgiveness causes our future relationships to suffer when we don't allow God to heal what is hurting us. We believe we have a right to be angry, but it's really our adversary trying to deceive us into staying offended.

God expects us to forgive. When it feels challenging or burdensome, we have the capacity to forgive. Not because others deserve it, but because we didn't deserve to be forgiven by God. Forgiveness affords us the opportunity to find true freedom and joy; bitterness is a prison. We believe that holding an account of wrongdoings is a way to "guard our hearts," but it actually allows our peace to slowly decay. It's unloving to hold someone's flaws against them when God never does that to us (1 Corinthians 13:5).

THE HARDEST TO FORGIVE

Many of you reading this may have no issue forgiving those who have hurt you. You're willing to love and release the pain where others have wounded you. You are willing to let go of the trauma and abuse you have endured. You're willing to give everyone the benefit of the doubt, but when it comes to yourself, you are your own biggest critic. You have never given yourself the grace you have extended to everyone else.

I have made so many mistakes that I believed were irreversible. Like Peter, I felt the many times I betrayed my Lord meant that I was no longer useful for His kingdom or His plan. Like Paul, I can boldly declare that I'm the worst of sinners—a young man who was deep in chains of perversion lust, inappropriate conversations, and raunchy connections. Someone aware of his calling to preach the gospel and share the love of Jesus, but who was still holding unforgiveness against those who betrayed him in his weakest moments. Thankfully, God has shown me that He never chose me because of my goodness. Nevertheless, I can also boast like Paul because people like me are exactly who Jesus came to save (Matthew 9:13; 1 Timothy 1:15). The hardest person to forgive at times can be ourselves. Yes, God forgives us, but sometimes we hold our mistakes against ourselves for longer than we should. I've learned that when God forgives us and we choose to not forgive ourselves, we are placing ourselves in a seat of judgment above God—and that is idolatry.

Jesus had twelve disciples, but he had three friends we can consider his inner circle—Peter, James, and John. I think we can definitely say that Peter was the outspoken one of the bunch. He was always willing to declare his love for Jesus and stand up to defend Him. In spite of his love for Jesus, he still denied Him when times were the worst. We read in Luke 22 and Matthew 26 that three times Peter decided to reject his connection to Jesus to preserve his own life, safeguarding himself. What made the situation more devastating for Peter is that Jesus forewarned him that he was going to deny Him three times. Peter wept bitterly after this happened because he knew he didn't deserve to be forgiven. He didn't earn the right to still be loved by Jesus. He knew he wasn't worthy to be a friend of Jesus if he would betray Him that way. Or so he thought.

Undeterred by the rejection, Jesus still reminded Peter that

He had a plan for his life. He still had a future beyond the betrayal. He still could be used for the glory of God because he was never selected due to his perfection. God knew his issues before he was born (Jeremiah 1:5). Peter was restored, and he preached one of the greatest messages ever at the birth of the church (Acts 2). We need to grasp what happened here. Peter wasn't just forgiven and allowed to attend weekend services. On the contrary, he was restored and allowed to lead others to Jesus. He went from rejecting Jesus to preaching about being filled with the Holy Spirit. You may have sins and issues in your life that you wish you never indulged in, but as long as you have Jesus, you have hope. You can be defined by what Jesus did on the cross, rather than the mistakes you've made. You can forgive others and yourself. There's no need to continue holding yourself hostage. The Word encourages us:

> If we say we have no sin, we deceive ourselves, and the truth is not in us. If we confess our sins, he is faithful and just to forgive us our sins, and to cleanse us from all unrighteousness. If we say we have not sinned, we make him a liar, and his word is not in us. (1 John 1:8–10 ESV)

The world tries to tell us that once we are broken, God is done with us. Cancel culture tells us that we must be spotless to be accepted. The Word of God shows us that God desires to be close to us despite our past. He is willing to forgive as we turn back to Him. God wants us all to be in harmony with one another (Romans 12:18). That originates with forgiveness. First

Corinthians 13 gives us a biblical definition of love, but I want to show you something special about true love. Verse 5 tells us "it keeps no record of being wronged." Godly love doesn't hold on to past offenses, but it seeks to bring reconciliation. Woke culture may dismiss you, but the grace of God will find you. If God can forgive you, it's time to forgive yourself. And if God is willing to give you a second chance, you have the ability to forgive those who offended you. A godly relationship isn't one that is devoid of problems, but it is a relationship with two individuals who have learned to extend that same mercy and grace to one another that Jesus has extended to them. To prepare for a thriving relationship, practice forgiveness in all areas of your life. Then you can go forward in freedom and lightness, not weighed down by baggage.

9

CONNECTED FOR PURPOSE

I (Safa) don't know if any of you love traveling, but we surely do. There's nothing like seeing beautiful places you have never been to before. Not to mention the authentic foods that are only local in that city! For most of the places we want to see, we have to get on a plane to visit. Unfortunately, some of those flights aren't nonstop flights. Sometimes we have to get a connecting flight before we reach our destination. One time I had to get on a connecting flight in Atlanta for my first time going to England, and navigating that major airport was one more thing to deal with on an already long-haul flight. That was a draining day.

These connecting flights help us get to our final destinations because sometimes planes have to stop to refuel or simply take other passengers somewhere else. While I love seeing new places,

I couldn't travel aimlessly. In my opinion, it's necessary to have a goal in mind. I need to know that if I get on these two planes, I'm going to end up somewhere I want to be.

When it comes to dating in this generation, I feel as though society pushes the notion that we should connect for fun. We aren't setting a goal of marriage or honoring God, but we are just together without a true purpose. Yes, dating can be fun, but it can have the same outcome as traveling without a purpose in view—wasted time.

Dating has become a very popular pastime in today's generation. Many people date not because they believe it's what God desires for their future but simply out of boredom—they need something to do. Marriage isn't the goal in mind, it just seems as though they should be dating. Pregnancy isn't the goal, but they are in bed together. A future together isn't what they're praying for, they just don't like being alone. When has dating turned from something we do purposefully to simply a hobby? Of course, the Bible doesn't mention anyone dating in the sense that we understand it in today's culture, but it does show us the beauty of marriage.

Two of the most important decisions we will ever make on this earth are surrendering our lives to Jesus and choosing the person to marry. When we started to take eternity seriously, many of us became born again (John 3:5). We started allowing God to free us from various sins and issues we used to wrestle with. But I think we often take our relationships lightly, as if they are meaningless. Is that what God intended? I don't think so.

I believe you're holding this book because you want your

current or future relationship to be God honoring. You want you and your significant other to lead one another closer to Jesus rather than straight to the bedroom. Do you feel God urging you toward a deeper walk with Him? Do you want a relationship with Him that isn't rooted in a to-do list and church attendance but in intimacy? If you feel God drawing you closer to Him, it's important that the person you connect to assists you in that process. Who you marry will help determine who you worship (1 Kings 11:4). Like a connecting flight, they will take you somewhere—and you want your final destination together to be located firmly in God's presence.

Every person you meet serves a purpose in some way—takes you in some direction. Unfortunately, many times it's not easy to tell why certain people are in our lives. Society has always encouraged us to find that picture-perfect person to date—someone who meets all our physical expectations and helps us make the most beautiful children. But there's so much more to dating: we need to approach it with our destination in mind. We need a relationship rooted in purpose. Let's discover how to have a purposeful relationship.

DO I HAVE THE RIGHT MOTIVES?

Can I (Tovares) be honest? There was a time when I felt like a loser because I was single. It's not that singleness is a curse; I actually found it to be a blessing. My problem was that all my boys used to make fun of me because they were sleeping around and I wasn't. It caused some insecurities that I couldn't shake for some time. I started aiming for relationships for two reasons: so I wouldn't get made fun of and so I could have fun without marriage in view.

What is it that drives you toward dating? Is it a Hollywood couple that inspires you? If so, I hope it's not a couple from one of these reality television shows who are only married for thirty-seven minutes. What about the YouTube vloggers? Their lives seem to be perfect, and you're wondering how they can be so blissful in Aruba while you're home eating Cheez-Its and waiting for your relationship to flourish. Are we interested in relationships because everyone else on our Instagram newsfeed is posting their couple pictures? You know people ignore your Bible verse quotes and pictures of your dog. But the moment they see a picture of a couple, *viral*! All the heart eyes.

Whatever the reason you're desiring marriage, you ought to have someone who is able to add to your life. Remember, God looked at Adam and realized that he needed a *helper* (Genesis 2). Many problems arise when we find someone who isn't actively helping us become who God called us to be. A counterfeit may bring happiness for a moment, but your relationship will bring you closer to God and true joy when God is the One who sends someone.

When it comes to dating, if we don't consider why we're connecting with someone, we are destined to end up in the arms of someone God didn't send. Not because we are foolish or we don't love God, but because our emotions can't lead us the way only God can.

Prior to marriage, I can honestly admit that I had very shallow requirements for what I desired in a wife. As a teenager, I would pray for God to send me a woman with a nice body. If she had what I considered a nice figure and attended church, she was automatically "wife material." Her personality could have been questionable, as long as I felt that she was beautiful. She didn't even have to be able to quote any verses. If she was attractive, she was "God's will" for my life. Please don't judge me. I was young and thirsty. Dehydrated, even! But I do know someone reading this is thinking exactly the way I did growing up. No, don't try to ignore this part. I'm talking to you, bro. You know you've been thirsty before as well, ladies. All of us have had moments when our list of demands was either unrealistic or shallow.

However, I have learned that passion is fickle, and we should pursue based on purpose instead. The problem with relationships led by our carnal desires is that if we have to sin in order to start them, we have to continue in sin to maintain them. In my immaturity, I placed a great emphasis on the curves of the woman rather than the character she possessed. That type of lustful thinking led me to make horrible decisions growing up. Chasing behind women without the leading of the Holy Spirit or godly counsel led me closer to bedrooms than to marriage. Now I'm not saying God isn't concerned about our preferences, or that having a "type" is a sin. God is not upset with you for desiring an attractive spouse. Thankfully, Safa far exceeded my expectations with her beauty and her character. What I'm saying is, it is possible to wrongly pursue someone based solely on passion rather than purpose. It's important that we as men pursue women with hearts for God rather than just curves, and that ladies find men who pursue Jesus above all else. If a man isn't being led by Jesus, it is impossible for him to help a woman get closer to Jesus. Or as Safa always tells young ladies when teaching, "Don't chase after the ring or the fairytale. Finding a man who loves God more than he loves you should be the foundation."

Remember, if you are like I was and charmed by looks, Proverbs 31:30 says, "Charm is deceptive, and beauty does not last; but a woman who fears the LORD will be greatly praised." That goes equally for both men and women. There are some people who look thirty and they're almost fifty-six, but for the most part, looks will fade. Things will sag. Wrinkles will change things. Hair will turn gray or fall out. Six-packs will turn into one-packs. If all someone sees in you is your beauty, you can be sure that the love will fade as the beauty fades. A relationship built on emotions cannot stand through trials and temptations. But someone who fears the Lord will be greatly praised.

THE IMPORTANCE OF PURPOSE

There was a king by the name of Xerxes who was looking for a new wife because his queen, Vashti, had offended him. His council thought that if word got out that the queen could disobey the king, wives everywhere would begin to revolt in the same manner. Talk about being insecure. Mordecai heard of the king's decree and brought his cousin Esther, whom he had raised, to the king's palace. No one was aware of her Jewish background because Mordecai told her not to mention it. When the king finally met her, he loved her more than the other women and named her queen instead of Vashti.

Despite all the romance going on in Esther's life, problems arose for the Jewish people. King Xerxes gave a man named Haman a high position in the kingdom, and Haman used his position to demand that people bow to him as he walked by. Mordecai didn't care to do it. Haman's anger made him want to kill not just Mordecai but all Jewish people.

> Mordecai sent this reply to Esther: "Don't think for a moment that because you're in the palace you will escape when all other Jews are killed. If you keep quiet at a time like this, deliverance and relief for the Jews will arise from some other place, but you and your relatives will die. Who knows if perhaps you were made queen for just such a time as this?" (Esther 4:13–14)

Mordecai was informing his cousin that she wouldn't be exempt from the wrath to come. At some point, Xerxes and Haman would learn of her nationality. Mordecai wanted Esther to know that she could choose to help her people, or they would have to expect God to deliver in another fashion. He was showing her the possibility that God ordained her marriage so she could protect the Jewish people when this moment came to pass. And due to her union, she was able to stop the attack on the children of Israel. If she hadn't been connected to the king, she would have had no say, and the Jewish people could've simply been destroyed by Haman's evil plan.

God connects us to certain people for a reason. When you're connected to the person God has for you, it will lead you closer to your purpose rather than away from it. Relationships that are focused on doing the will of God also benefit the lives of the people around them. Let's be honest: many of us would've been content being royalty. Imagine being like Esther and marrying the man many women coveted, and ending up with all types of blessings: money, fame, power, and more. Isn't that like what social media tells us to do? Focus on getting married to the attractive guy or the beautiful woman. Post pictures as you two travel the world. We hear less about how marriages should push us to serve instead of being served. We hear more about being invested in the wedding day than about how a godly marriage should look. When connected to the right relationship, you will be able to bring glory to God. Not only will you have the opportunity to serve one another, you can be sure that your union will be an example to the world of what true love looks like.

As I've mentioned before, Safa and I were raised in the church, but many of you weren't afforded the opportunity to be brought up in Christianity. You may have had an idea of who Jesus was, but you didn't know Him personally. You may not have had the type of family who would help disciple you at home and show you examples of what Christianity should look like outside of the four walls of a church. Connecting to the right person gives you the chance to break those generational curses and form new healthy, holy habits in your home. Remember the life of Rahab. Everyone knew she had been a prostitute in her past, but what did that matter after she protected the Israelite spies in Joshua 2? God changed her future because of one divine connection. Eventually, Rahab married Salmon, and they gave birth to Boaz later on. David was a descendant from her lineage as well—and ultimately Jesus Christ Himself. God didn't allow her sexual baggage to stop her from being in line with the plans God had for our earth.

When God has great plans for your life, He connects you to the right people. We find the type of relationships in which people will cover us spiritually, challenge us when they see areas we can grow in, and correct us when we may be off track or we're just not living up to the standard God has for us. Conversely, when the Enemy wants to destroy our lives, he sends the wrong people our way, people who will lure us into sin, keep us comfortable doing things outside of God's will, or try to criticize us whenever we seek to please God with our lives. Consider the purpose of your relationships and where your connections are taking you.

THE ONE

A common misconception has crept its way into the church. It may not be sinful to believe this, but it sure can be harmful and somewhat unrealistic. Many believe that they have a "soul mate" out there who will complete them and cause them to live happily ever after once they're married. There won't be any effort needed. There will be no arguments. You will have clarity from day one, and you'll have doves show up at your wedding singing "hallelujah!" God may even speak to them through several confirmations, and there will be no doubt that this is the person God has for you.

All those things would be lovely, but they aren't necessarily biblical. It sounds more like a Disney special or some weird Lifetime movie where we know the couple gets married in the end, and we are given the idea that they will live happily ever after. Unfortunately, movies typically end right at that blissful moment. We don't see the chaos after the boy gets the girl. We don't see how the relationship failed in a couple of months. Netflix may show some amazing films, but they do not often show what happens in reality. Reality TV doesn't even show the struggles couples face. They only show the highlight reels or staged interactions that keep the ratings high.

While I am convinced that my wife is the person God desired for me, I believe that ultimately Jesus is our actual "soul mate." Hollywood pushes a narrative that all we have to do is find the perfect person and we will live happily ever after. But that isn't what we find in the Scriptures. It's simply hard to believe that God won't force us to worship Him, but He will force us to marry one specific person or else we won't be able to walk in His will. It's not necessarily the person we marry who causes us to be in God's will or not. Instead, because we are walking in obedience to Christ, He is leading us to make the right decision in who we marry. The Bible says to acknowledge Him in everything we do, because then He will direct our paths (Proverbs 3:5–6). So instead of finding "the one," we need to ensure we are becoming "the one" ourselves—that we're becoming someone worth marrying and that we're growing into our purpose.

God in all His sovereign wisdom still allows for something called *free will*. Not that He doesn't know what we will do, but He allows us to make decisions. As believers, our focus should be staying in the presence of God so we choose someone who loves Jesus and complements us. I believe someone becomes "the one" the moment we say, "I do." That is when we entrust our relationship to God's covenant, to love and cherish them despite other options.

THE TRUE GOAL OF MARRIAGE

When I (Safa) was studying in college, those were some of the most tedious moments of my life. I felt that because of my difficult major, biomedical science, I had to study while others could slack off. When everyone was watching movies or at every sporting event, I would be catching up on my homework. I knew that in order to excel, I would have to stay focused on my grades more than anything else.

As much as I am embarrassed to admit it, there were many times I would study to pass the test rather than to understand the material. Unfortunately, that information overload never truly allowed me to grasp what the teacher was saying; it only helped me pass the class. This always negatively impacts us, though, because we will end up graduating and not fully understanding what we studied. After graduation, you're expected to be able to apply the information you just learned, especially if you're in a field like medicine or engineering. But you won't be able to do that if you mishandled your season of learning.

Many times we forget about the true purpose of marriage, and that explains why we mishandle the season of singleness. When I was single, I aimed to be intentional during my single season. There were many opportunities to date, but I focused more on growing spiritually before a relationship, discovering my calling, ensuring I took my college education seriously, and spending time connecting with friends. My desire was to not waste my singleness or think my life's purpose began after "I do." Remember, the main focus of marriage should always be giving glory to God, not discovering yourself. It should be a union built on purpose instead of feelings. It's important to have the right mindset when approaching marriage because not doing so will cause us to settle for a connection that doesn't glorify God.

First Corinthians 10:31 says, "Whether you eat or drink, or whatever you do, do it all for the glory of God." When we are focused on bringing glory to God, we won't settle for what's convenient. If you are single in today's culture, I know that it can be somewhat exhausting. You're probably feeling left out. Everyone appears to be in a relationship. Even your neighbor's pet dog seems to get attention, while you're alone. But when you know your worth, settling isn't an option. When you know that your mindset is pleasing God, that will surely narrow your options away from those who are simply seeking fun. When we keep a kingdom mindset, we choose to not settle for someone who simply catches our eye, but we desire the type of relationship that builds our spirit and helps us get closer to our purpose. Our main goal must be purpose, not passion.

PURPOSE OUTWEIGHS PASSION

The first time I (Tovares) saw Safa, it was a moment I'll never forget. But seeing how beautiful she was didn't make her marriage material. Initially, I pursued her because I found her physically attractive. However, I am thankful that God protected her from me. God knew my immature and lustful ways wouldn't have been beneficial to her life, so He didn't allow it to work the first time I tried. We remained friends through the years, but I noticed that the girls I entertained after meeting Safa weren't working out how I thought they would.

I realized later that those relationships couldn't work, because I was connecting to those women out of lust and other superficial reasons. I learned firsthand that if your relationship doesn't have God as the foundation, it won't last. Purpose outweighs passion. So, while I was immaturely praying, "God, send me a Christian woman with a nice body," He ensured that He sent a woman after His heart. Her outer beauty was simply icing on the cake.

When relationships reach hard times, and they will, we need to be with someone who will lead us back to Jesus. Society makes us think the dream marriage is the one with many vacations, a large bank account, and a nice social media aesthetic. Those aren't necessarily bad goals to have, but what God desires for your future is much bigger than that. Do you want to see your home abiding by the teachings Jesus left to the apostles, or will you settle for a family that follows culture and doesn't know who Jesus really is?

When Abraham was ready to find a spouse for his son Isaac,

he sent his servant on a quest to get the job done (Genesis 24). He made the servant swear that he wouldn't get a woman from the land they were in, Canaan, but that he would find a woman from their native land. I want you to understand what Abraham was really saying here. He didn't want his son to find an ungodly relationship simply because it was more convenient. He didn't want his son to mingle with the women involved in practices that didn't please God. Abraham knew that it was wiser to travel a far distance to find a spouse who pleased God than to jump into a relationship out of lust or convenience.

Are there single people around you who you feel aren't going to help you serve God? Don't settle simply to feel relieved of the waiting period. Now, I'm not talking about the imperfect people who are striving to please Jesus, because none of us is perfect. I mean the relationships that are showing you more red flags than a carnival. It's the will of God for you to trust His timing rather than manufacture your own plan and try to add God to it later on. Our plans fail when emotions are guiding us rather than the Spirit of Christ.

WHERE IS YOUR RELATIONSHIP HEADED?

Jesus taught His disciples that they'd know a tree by the fruit it produces (Matthew 7:20). We've already talked about looking for fruit in the life of someone we're interested in. But once we're dating someone, if we truly want to know if our relationship is purposeful and ordained by God, we'll examine the fruit of that relationship. We'll evaluate the steps we have been making since the connection formed. We know that God may be at the source when our spiritual life is propelling forward and we are being molded into the image of Christ. But if you find yourself constantly out of alignment with the Word of God, it's a clear indicator to reevaluate.

Ask: *Am I closer to Jesus? Am I being strengthened and helping them grow as well? Are they following Jesus for themselves, or are they just attending church to be close to me? Is this relationship maintaining biblical boundaries? Are we forgiving one another and extending grace like Christ has done for us?* These are the questions we need to ask to see if we are connected by the Holy Spirit or are being led by our emotions.

Choosing a spouse will influence the rest of your life. It's important that you find someone you're compatible with and attracted to, but please ensure you find someone who is able to fit where God is taking you. We know God has a calling on our lives, and we need someone who can help us get there. A relationship built on purpose is a relationship that doesn't crumble when adversity hits—it strengthens you. When a couple is purpose driven, you can see true love and acceptance. King Xerxes and Esther had a union that protected the Jewish people. A marriage like that of Joseph and Mary, the parents of Jesus, is another example. When society would have told Joseph to disown Mary and not believe her story about how she became pregnant, God came in the flesh to save humanity. Anything is possible when God is the One who orchestrates your union.

Throughout this book, we've revealed to you some of the

most important principles we've learned about dating and some of the most urgent questions we receive from followers of Godly Dating 101. We've told you the truth about what we've been through. We've talked about the best foundation for love. We've talked about community—who you want to welcome on your team. We've talked about the nature of the human heart and the truth about sex. We've explored the blessings that come from having healthy boundaries and how to tell a counterfeit Christian from the real deal when looking for a mate. We've delved into the critical concept of forgiveness, and we hope we've armed you to go forward in dating with your purpose in mind.

But most of all, we want to make sure you return to the presence of God over and over, because He is what makes it happen. Everything else is secondary. Follow God first, and you'll find yourself where you need to be in your life and in your dating relationships.

Wherever you are in your dating journey, we invite you to Godly Dating 101 on social media, where you can continue to connect with us and others who are seeking real, honest answers about dating in today's world in a way that honors God. Don't stop learning, and don't stop seeking. It's okay to follow the truth of God's Word instead of being influenced by the pressures of what our culture is saying.

While it might feel like you're going against the grain or counter to culture as you seek to date in a godly way, you're not alone. Keep fighting, keep seeking His will, and keep walking forward in strength, knowing that we are behind you and God's people are supporting you. No matter how slim your options may seem, there are many people out there who are aiming to date in a way that honors Christ and isn't heading toward sin.

When you find the strength of a godly relationship, you bring glory to Him and more love, joy, and purpose to this world. Isn't that what we all want? Waiting can feel frustrating, but when God blesses you, you will see that His blessings are worth the wait.

Writing this book has been a dream come true. We encounter so many believers, young and old, who are always searching for answers when it comes to dating. Our aim is that this book will point us back to the Bible to see God's truth about relationships and that our ears will be opened to the voice of God, instead of what society thinks is normal.

It is our prayer that going forward, this book will do more than encourage someone to pursue marriage. We desire for you to pursue Christ above all. Being married is amazing, but it won't fulfill us if we aren't in alignment with what God desires for us. As you pursue His will, don't allow culture or emotions to rush you off course.

ACKNOWLEDGMENTS

Merely acknowledging you all isn't enough for what you've done for us. This book exists because God used all of you to pull this out of us.

To know what the Bible says about love is one thing, but to see it exemplified by you, Patrick and Joan, is truly a blessing. Having godly parents is amazing. You two always said I would impact this world. God heard your prayers. You have always supported my dreams and visions. Thank you for believing when I didn't.

To my (Safa) parents, Norman and Mervilyn, you have always taught me to go after my dreams and supported me in the pursuit of whatever that might have looked like. Because of you I have learned I can accomplish anything I put my mind to.

To Steven Scarlett who mentored me (Tovares) and remained patient with me for many years. There is no Godly Dating 101 ministry or book without your years of investment.

ACKNOWLEDGMENTS

To our Banner of Love and EMAC family, you all were paramount to our spiritual foundation. You did everything possible to teach us the truth of God's Word, and we wouldn't be able to write books or help others if you didn't first pour into us since we were children. Godly leadership is something we have never taken for granted.

To Tom Dean, our agent, who saw something great in us and helped make this book a reality. You are a great friend, and we appreciate you.

The dream team over at W Publishing—you all are second to none! You've embraced us and believed in our message. You all were great to work with—especially Kyle! Thankful you were more than an editor but a strong support system when the process didn't feel easy.

And finally, to everyone in our extended family who has supported Godly Dating 101 over all of these years. Thank you for believing in our voice as we spoke the things of God, despite society telling us we had to conform in order to make a difference. This book is for you!

NOTES

CHAPTER 1: GODLY DATING IS PREPARATION FOR MARRIAGE

1. Zack Friedman, "49% of Millennials Would Quit Their Job Within 2 Years," *Forbes*, May 22, 2019, https://www.forbes.com /sites/zackfriedman/2019/05/22/millennials-disillusioned-future /?sh= ef0ff04353ea.
2. Shellie R. Warren, "10 Most Common Reasons for Divorce," Marriage.com, updated September 30, 2021, https://www .marriage.com/advice/divorce/10-most-common-reasons-for -divorce/.
3. John Maxwell, quoted in Dave Ramsey, The Money Answer Book (Nashville: Thomas Nelson, 2010), 87.

CHAPTER 2: A FOUNDATION FOR TRUE LOVE

1. Joe Hernandez, "One of the Deadliest U.S. Accidental Structural Collapses Happened 40 Years Ago Today," NPR News, July 17, 2021, https://www.npr.org/2021/07/17 /1016603199/one-of-the-deadliest-u-s-accidental-structural -collapses-happened-40-years-ago-t.

CHAPTER 5: THE TRUTH ABOUT SEX

1. Stephanie Kramer, "US Has World's Highest Rate of Children Living in Single-Parent Households," Pew Research Center, December 12, 2019, https://www.pewresearch.org/fact-tank /2019/12/12/u-s-children-more-likely-than-children-in-other -countries-to-live-with-just-one-parent/.

2. Adrienne Santos-Longhurst, "Why Is Oxytocin Known as the 'Love Hormone'? And 11 Other FAQs," Healthline, August 30, 2018, https://www.healthline.com/health/love-hormone.

3. "How Does the Porn Industry Make Money Today?" Fight the New Drug, April 13, 2021, https://fightthenewdrug.org/how -does-the-porn-industry-actually-make-money-today/.

4. "How Porn Can Affect the Brain Like a Drug," Fight the New Drug, May 11, 2021, https://fightthenewdrug.org/how-porn-can -affect-the-brain-like-a-drug/.

ABOUT THE AUTHORS

Tovares Grey is a believer, husband of Safa, and father of two. He is a social media content creator that focuses his work on Christianity and relationships. Tovares has always had a passion for serving and helping people find hope, joy, and intimacy with Jesus despite what life may be throwing their way. He started the Godly Dating 101 ministry in 2012 as a single individual trying to learn how to date God's way and help others on that journey as well. As a Christian content creator, he has a burden to share with his generation the benefits of honoring Christ in all of our decisions. He is a U.S. Navy veteran and currently resides in Tampa, Florida, where he is pursuing a master's degree in health administration at the University of South Florida.

Safa Grey has always had a passion for writing, through journaling and poetry specifically. Others know her by her singing ability as she's always been a praise and worship leader in her local church. Growing up, writing always provided her an outlet for her prayers and expressing herself. Because she herself did not always have a young female role model in her adolescent youth, Safa is determined to always help young ladies who are in the same shoes she was in. As a Christian content creator, Safa has a desire to help young adults find their worth in Christ rather than the opinions of modern culture. She was born in Jamaica and now resides in Tampa, Florida, with her husband, Tovares, and their two children.